Dialogue and Disagreement

Franz Rosenzweig's Relevance to Contemporary Jewish–Christian Understanding

Ronald H. Miller

Foreword by Rabbi Yechiel Eckstein

UNIVERSITY
PRESS OF
AMERICA

Lanham • New York • London

Copyright © 1989 by

University Press of America,® Inc.

4720 Boston Way
Lanham, MD 20706

3 Henrietta Street
London WC2E 8LU England

British Cataloging in Publication Information Available

Library of Congress Cataloging-in-Publication Data

Miller, Ronald Henry.
Dialogue and disagreement : Franz Rosenzweig's relevance to
contemporary Jewish–Christian understanding / by Ronald H. Miller ;
foreword by Yechiel Eckstein.
p.   cm.
Bibliography: p.
Includes index.
1. Rosenzweig, Franc, 1886–1929. 2. Judaism—Relations—Christianity—
1945–   . 3. Christianity and other religions—Judaism—1945–   .
I. Title.
BM755.R6M54   1989   296.3'872—dc20   89–35492 CIP

ISBN 0–8191–7539–0 (alk. paper)
ISBN 0–8191–7549–8 (pbk. : alk. paper)

The paper used in this publication meets the minimum requirements of American
National Standard for Information Sciences—Permanence of Paper for Printed Library
Materials, ANSI Z39.48–1984.   ∞

In memory of my mother
Alvina Klein Miller
May 26, 1907 - February 8, 1985
with love and gratitude

TABLE OF CONTENTS

FOREWORD
by

RABBI YECHIEL ECKSTEIN
HOLYLAND FELLOWSHIP OF
CHRISTIANS AND JEWS

Last year marked a personal milestone in my life. A decade had passed since I first began my professional activities advancing Christian-Jewish relations. I celebrated the occasion by engaging in a serious *cheshbon hanefesh*, the Hebrew term for reflection or soul searching. I realized that the greatest joy and fulfillment from my job over the years came from the friendships I had made, and that my ten year relationship with Ron Miller was not only the longest, but also the deepest and most satisfying. In the course of this decade, we have shared with one another life's triumphs and struggles. We have cried together tears of joy and sorrow. We have spoken of our faith, our pain, our doubts. Like Damon and Phythias, like David and Jonathan, we have entrusted to each other some of our deepest fears and our innermost concerns. We have watched each other's children grow up as we ourselves entered into middle age. We have spent evening upon evening and day upon day being symbiotically nurtured from each other's knowledge, experience, and insight. And, though he would deny it, I have been the primary beneficiary in the relationship.

Franz Rosenzweig, who was fortunate to have had a similar kind of relationship with Hans Ehrenberg, writes that their friendship was maintained through all the vicissitudes of travel and time. Like

them, Ron and I were "destined to orbit together as
sister planets." Over all these years, however, we
walked down separate, albeit parallel, paths--he as a
Christian, I as a Jew.

   I write here of these sentiments, not only because they are true and personally meaningful, but
because I became aware that the relationship Ron and
I have enjoyed for over a decade was, in fact, paradigmatic of what we were both trying to achieve in our
careers or "ministries"--namely, a new spirit of understanding between Christians and Jews. Both Ron and I
have devoted ourselves to fostering, not only tolerance
and respect between our two communities, but genuine
dialogue and even love. Moreover, we have both done
so without asking either community to compromise its
core convictions, nor have we done so ourselves in the
microcosmic relationship of our own lives. Indeed, we
have found that Rabbi Heschel's pithy dictum, "faith
must precede interfaith" held true. The secret to our
friendship lies in the fact that we each *affirm* our
particular faith--he as a Christian, I as a Jew. Like
the ideal we both strive to achieve on a collective level,
our relationship has been a living dialogue in the truest
sense.

   Readers of this wonderful book should not be
surprised that it was Franz Rosenzweig who, more than
any other Jewish thinker, early captured Ron's imagination and scholarly interest. In his personal life, as well
as in his writing and teaching, Ron has long attempted
to live out the vision of dialogue and relationship that
Rosenzweig ascribed to and wrote about so eloquently.

   As a teacher beloved by his students, Ron has
enlightened the minds of hundreds, nay thousands, of
people, Christians and Jews, young and old, and opened
them up to a greater reality and transcendence. While
I, in my capacity as Director of the Holyland Fellowship
of Christians and Jews, was always overly concerned
with affecting the masses, numbers were never his preoccupation. With him, what was important was the
quality of the relationships he was engaging in and the

kind of model he was serving for others. Yet the numbers came inevitably, despite his not pursuing them--perhaps because he did not. He has uplifted his students with his wisdom and left an indelible imprint on their lives with his love.

Rosenzweig's life and vision--as well as Ron's--are captured beautifully in this very readable, scholarly book. In the **first chapter**, the reader will learn about the life, writings, and thought of one of the greatest Jewish thinkers of the 20th century--a man who regarded Judaism as his own path of faith but who viewed Christianity as a true religion that brought people into an authentic covenantal relationship with God. Rosenzweig is a model for Christians and Jews alike.   He was both a religious individual and a thoroughly modern man; he was deeply committed to his faith and community, yet always open and engaging towards others who did not share his perspective. Indeed, Rosenzweig was "the prototype of the modern man of faith living between the alternatives of an absolute changing belief and a dogmatically closed unbelief." His starting point, as is true for all people of faith, was in paying attention to reality.   "The beginning of faithfulness lies in doing whatever is at hand to do, but with a readiness for meeting God.   Every moment contains the possibility of encountering the divine."

The casual observer may ask why, in a book containing only five chapters, two are devoted to the subject of revelation.   Yet for Rosenzweig, "the crucial theological source of a new paradigm for understanding Judaism and Christianity both in themselves and in their relationship to each other" lies in this doctrine of revelation. The **second chapter** traces the idea of revelation in Rosenzweig's early writings.   The **third chapter** focuses on the role of revelation in *The Star of Redemption*.   The reader comes to appreciate the crucial importance of Rozenzweig's revelational theology, understanding how a noncognitive theory of revelation allows for a theology of Judaism that accepts the truth of Christianity and a theology of Christianity that witnesses to the enduring truth of Judaism.

Perhaps more importantly, the reader comes to appreciate that ideas do not arise in a vacuum but germinate from life experiences and relationships. Nowhere is this more apparent in this book than in the **fourth chapter** where the English-speaking reader encounters for the first time Rosenzweig's extensive correspondence with his· cousin, close friend, and dialogical partner, Hans Ehrenberg, a Jewish convert to Christianity. The inexorable link between life and thought, with each nurturing the other, and both emerging from a commitment to pursue "I-Thou" relationships with both God and human beings, is the thread that runs through this chapter. Authentic dialogue is seen as the common, sanctified ground Christians and Jews share and on which they can hopefully meet.

The book does not end with Rosenzweig's death in 1929. Dr. Miller, thoroughly trained in Roman Catholic theology, employs Rosenzweig's insights to open up for us in the **fifth chapter** the whole path of contemporary Jewish-Christian understanding with his reflections on some of the official statements and promulgations emanating from Christian sources, especially the pronouncements of the Roman Catholic Church since the Second Vatican Council. Discussion of these documents leads him to reflect on the primary source of Christian consciousness of Jews in the letters of Paul. I found the author's thoughtful and penetrating discussion of Paul, someone he has studied for over twenty years, especially informative and provocative.

This is a book in which the appendices are not to be neglected. I was privileged to attend the day of dialogue that is the subject of **Appendix A**. Here we find the author in dialogue with one of Rosenzweig's students, the eminent scholar Dr. Nahum Glatzer, and with Rabbi Robert Marx, a Reform rabbi. **Appendix B** embodies the principles of Jewish-Christian relations developed so carefully in the book. It is here that we see the concrete details of the dialogical work pursued by Ron Miller for almost fifteen years now through Common Ground, the center for interfaith study and dialogue which he founded and continues to co-direct.

For whom then is this book intended? For readers who have never met Franz Rosenzweig. For those who have studied Rosenzweig 's writings currently available in English but who do not read the original German text of his letters and essays. For those who are interested in Jewish-Christian dialogue today: its roots, its history, and its ongoing reality. For those involved in dialogue at various levels of community life. For all of those who want to read a book that will both inform and transform them in their understanding of the shared journey of discovery stretching out before Jews and Christians alike in these last years of the 20th century.

The words of Psalm 73 carved on Rosenzweig's tombstone, "*Ani tamid imach*," ("I am always with You") is not only a beautiful description of Rosenzweig's relationship with God; it is also the legacy both he and one of his greatest Christian disciples ever, Ron Miller, challenge us with today and for years to come.

PREFACE

Jung calls it synchronicity; to most of us it would simply be a matter of following a hunch. I was walking along a street in Kassel, taking some slides of Rosenzweig's home city on a return trip to Germany some six years after I had lived there as a student. I had thought that my photographic opportunities in this city were exhausted--having taken several pictures of the lovely home Rosenzweig's parents had acquired on the outskirts of Kassel when Franz was 26--when a lithograph store uncannily attracted me. Not really knowing why I was there, I requested lithographs from 1905, the year Franz had completed his secondary education. When questioned about this particular choice of a year, I explained the nature of my visit to Kassel. The shopkeeper gave me the name and telephone number of a friend of his who had an interest in Rosenzweig; I called him directly from the store. He was not only home and interested but also gave me another name and telephone number, this time of an archivist with access to records saved from Rosenzweig's high school, the Friedrichsgymnasium, destroyed along with two-thirds of the city in a bombing attack on October 22, 1943. This gentleman told me that Rosenzweig's wife was currently in Berlin working on a forthcoming edition of her husband's works. He gave me both telephone numbers--for the archivist in Kassel and for Frau Edith Scheinmann-Rosenzweig in Berlin. It was with two leads far more valuable than lithographs that I left this store I had found by "chance."

Having decided to extend my stay in Kassel, I called the archivist and was invited to visit her the next day. She showed me the list of the topics on

which the eighteen-year old Franz had been examined
for his *Abitur*, the diploma enabling one to pursue a
university career. She also showed me the list of the
nineteen students in his graduating class with their
names, birth dates, religious affiliations, fathers' occu-
pations, and their own chosen vocational goals. Franz
was one of five Jewish students in his class; their
religious identity was not signified by *jüdisch* (Jewish)
but *israelitisch* (Israelite). His father's profession was
listed as businessman and his vocational goal was
medicine (which he did study for awhile in his early
university career, moving later to history and finally to
philosophy).

I photocopied both lists and pored over them that
evening in my hotel room. I knew what had happened
to Rosenzweig but I wondered about the fate of those
other young Jewish graduates: Kurt Rothfels and Hugo
Hess who wanted to study law; Karl Sichel whose goal
was to be an architect; Fritz Tobias who hoped to be a
doctor. How haunting such simple lists become in the
wake of the Holocaust. Yet the Jewish identity and
aspirations of these high school graduates seemed so
natural and secure in the Germany of 1905.

These thoughts were still in my head as I sat on
the train the next day bound for Berlin. Having found
a hotel, I called the number of Frau Scheinmann-Rosenzweig's apartment. It seemed strange to be calling the
wife of a man who had died in 1929, a woman twice
widowed (her second marriage was to Dr. Scheinmann),
a refugee from Hitler's Germany who had escaped to
Israel, a woman now eighty-one years old (if the husband of her youth had been alive that afternoon of
March 22, 1976 he would have been ninety). My rever-
ies were interrupted by the cultured and dignified voice
of Mrs. Rosenzweig. I explained that I was finishing a
dissertation on her husband's thought and asked if I
might visit her. I was invited to coffee. Quickly
purchasing a bouquet of flowers (an indispensable part
of German etiquette), I hailed a cab and found myself
very shortly thereafter at her apartment.

She greeted me with a gracious smile, a handsome woman with penetrating dark eyes and gray hair parted in the middle and combed tightly back from her temples. Her modest attire matched the almost austere apartment. Despite her warmth, there was a "no nonsense" atmosphere about herself and her surroundings. She served *Kaffee und Kuchen* and showed me a number of Rosenzweig's letters which she was currently editing. I specifically remember picking up and reading the famous letter of October 31, 1913 to his cousin and close friend Rudolf Ehrenberg, when Rosenzweig informed him that he would not be converting to Christianity after all but would remain a Jew.

She told me she had three reasons for taking on this extensive work. First, it kept her close to a most treasured part of her past. Secondly, she felt it was something she could give posthumously to Franz. Thirdly, she added with a smile, this seemed a much better alternative to most of the activities with which old ladies kept busy. Her work has subsequently borne fruit; several volumes of Rosenzweig's *Gesammelte Schriften* are currently available through Nijhoff Publishers in Holland, books I have used extensively in preparing this manuscript.

As our conversation progressed she seemed to relax, especially when she realized I would not ask the indiscreet questions to which some interviewers had subjected her. She even suggested that we speak my native language for awhile and moved very effortlessly into fluent English. I declined her later offer to converse for a time in Hebrew, something for which a summer in Israel and basic Hebrew courses did not equip me. She began to reminisce about her first meeting with Franz when she was twelve and he was twenty-one. Their families had known each other and Franz came to be a regular Sabbath evening guest of the Hahns after his enrollment at the University of Berlin. In the beginning she was so young that she would be sent to bed just when the after-dinner conversations were getting interesting; but he kept coming to visit and she kept growing up. Soon she was allowed to stay up for those coveted conversations and after a few more years they were engaged.

At some point our conversation slipped back into German. She explained to me that she still considered herself a Berliner, even after the Nazi atrocities. Franz, of course, was already dead when she fled to Israel with their young son Rafael. She showed me a scrapbook her grandchildren in Israel had sent her (Rafael's family was living in Tel Aviv). The book was filled with quotes from the Hebrew translation of Rosenzweig's major work, *The Star of Redemption*. On the cover was a child's drawing of a branch of roses, the meaning of the German word *Rosenzweig*.

She encouraged me to finish my dissertation on Rosenzweig. She seemed especially enthused about Christians like myself being interested in his work and said that to the end of his life he believed that Christianity was a true religion, representing an authentic covenantal relationship with God. Of course, he also believed that there was no need for Jews to convert to Christianity, anymore than for Christians to convert to Judaism.

I was sad in saying goodbye to her. I wanted to take her picture or ask her some of those questions about Franz as a person which I think she might have judged indiscreet. I knew enough of German reticence and inwardness to respect her privacy. She was, after all, a Berliner. She told me that I might visit the university, now in East Berlin, where Franz had studied. Soberly she added that under communism the university was not really there anymore; only the buildings remained.

We corresponded. She wrote me in response to my plans for a Rosenzweig conference honoring the fiftieth anniversary of his death; the actual *Jahrzeit* date was December 10, 1979. She complained at that time of her failing health and included her new address in Baden Baden. The next correspondence I received from that address was a black-bordered notification of her death on November 15, 1979. She was eighty-four years old. I wish now that I could have given her a copy of this book, a small *Gastgeschenk* for the lovely afternoon we spent together in Berlin.

Ronald H. Miller

ACKNOWLEDGEMENTS

I would like to acknowledge with gratitude those who have helped me in the preparation of this manuscript: Rabbi Manfred Vogel, my teacher and constant source of inspiration and encouragement; Rabbi Marc Gellman, who helped me in my first understanding of the Jewish heart; Rabbi Yechiel Eckstein, whose friendship means a continuing participation in Judaism's innermost soul; Dr. Nahum Glatzer for his counsel and support, and his kind permission to publish the proceedings of the *Jahrzeit* conference; Rabbi Robert Marx for his participation in that same conference and for many hours of patient dialogue; Dr. Anne Jaron Brandt, a native of Frankfurt, who generously agreed to check all my translations from the German text of Rosenzweig; Lake Forest College and the Michael A. Posen foundation for grant monies which helped in the preparation of this volume; Kluwer Academic Publishers for permission to translate materials from the Rosenzweig *Gesammelte Schriften*; Rafael Rosenzweig for reading parts of the manuscript and encouraging this project; Linda Dunn, who assisted in the final preparation of the manuscript, both as typist and theological consultant; Harriet Doud, who patiently proofread the manuscript; talented student assistants at Lake Forest College--Dwight Buchholz, Noreen Curran, Jack Horn, Tom Meier, Lori Pierce, Jennifer Quinn, Christine Roby, Ed Wingenbach, and Scott Wright; my long-time friend and colleague, Jim Kenney, for his careful review of this text; the entire Common Ground community for promoting and nurturing my efforts to create dialogue; finally, my wonderful life-partner, Sherry, and our three beautiful children--Meredith, Jim, and Carrie--who distract me so often from my books and remind me that even study finds its final meaning in life.

CHAPTER ONE

A MODERN MAN
AND A JEW

A MAN

The pages turn stiffly in our hand, leaves from an old photo album, an imaginary one which helps us to focus on this remarkable man. It is not really that long ago. Perhaps the pictures seem so distant in space and time because the world to which they belong has largely disappeared. It was called *Deutschjudentum*, German Jewry. Apart from this Jewish community which considered itself (and indeed was) German, Franz Rosenzweig can never be understood. For this only child of Georg and Adele Rosenzweig was the proud scion of an educated, cultured, affluent German Jewish family. Today *Deutschjudentum* is mostly a memory, but in Rosenzweig's life and thought it will always find a flowering.

Franz's participation in German culture was unfeigned. Referring in 1916 to his projected publications, he wrote to his friend Eugen Rosenstock: "I have a deep sense of gratitude towards German culture. If it receives my gifts--to quote Homer, 'modest but lovely'---that is fine; if it does not receive them, that is fine too. . . ."[1] Bernhard Casper believes that the autobiographical testimonies of Rosenzweig constitute what might indeed be the richest account we have of the living symbiosis of German and Jew during the period of Imperial Germany and the Weimar Republic. In Rosenzweig one can see the ripest fruit of the grafting of Judaism and Germanism in a cultural and intellec-

1

tual life unparalleled in modern history. A reader of
the Rosenzweig *corpus* finds himself confronting the
almost unbelievable reality "that here a Jew of the
generation that was gassed in the death camps of the
Third Reich strove with all the powers of his heart to
be completely Jewish *and* completely German."[2]

We first turn to a picture from 1897; young
Franz is eleven years old. We see an earnest school-
boy, smartly dressed with sober mien, a shock of hair
rising from a high forehead, a well-proportioned face--
but, most of all, extraordinarily open and trusting eyes
staring out at a world still largely unknown. Margarete
Susman writes that she once heard Rosenzweig remark
while looking at one of these childhood pictures: "If
anyone could remain like that, he would never have
any need at all to write."[3]

Our next picture shows us a handsome young
scholar in the new home acquired by his family in
1904. Franz has decorated his large bedroom in the
popular *art nouveau* fashion and he sits writing at his
desk. Perhaps we see him writing the poem without
title or dedication which appears in his diary from this
same year:

> Dear God, who art on earth,
> Fill me with strength and desire.
> No sightseer's stroll through creation for me.
> Let me seize it with spirit on fire.
>
> Teach me, as never before, this earth
> To permeate and subdue with creative heart.
> Oh nature, not your glistening buds
> But your ripe fruit I choose as my part.
>
> Oh summer, greening in beauty,
> Standing witness to everything's end,
> I hope that you are considering
> Summer power my way to send.[4]

It is not a person but a place which provides the subject of the next picture. We see the city of Kassel, the lovely center of Rosenzweig's life until the inception of his university career. A steep tram ride takes one to the spacious Park Wilhelmshöhe where Rosenzweig often visited the impressive castle, the Hercules monument, and the extensive gardens with their magnificent view of the thousand-year-old city below."[5] The first steam-propelled streetcar in Europe was built here just a few years before Rosenzweig's birth and now carried people regularly to this scenic park. It was in the castle there that Rosenzweig's father and other members of the business community once met with the Kaiser.[6]

In the art gallery of Park Wilhelmshöhe one can still visit the monumental Rembrandt canvas depicting Jacob's blessing of Ephraim and Manasseh. Towards the end of his life, Rosenzweig wrote to August Mühlhausen that his earliest acquaintance with great painting was with this home-town treasure. He goes on to say: "Even today I surprise myself in realizing that the word *picture* calls up for me the 'Blessing of Jacob' housed in Kassel, just as for most people the word might cause them to think of the Sistine Madonna."[7] He continues in typical fashion, discussing whether the painting should be understood from a Christian viewpoint. He rejects this view since such a perspective is usually based on Jacob's crossed hands which is an element in the *Genesis* text actually omitted from the Rembrandt painting.[8]

Turning back now to our album, we find Rosenzweig in his student quarters at one or other of the university centers he attended in those halcyon days before World War I. From Munich, where he was studying medicine, the young romantic writes to his parents: "I wish I were a symphony by Beethoven, or else something else that has been completely written. What hurts is the process of being written. Given my choice I would want to be tonight's, the B-flat Major."[9]

A memorable picture of the twenty-two-year old Franz emerges from the memory of his friend, Hermann Badt. Rosenzweig was staying in Hain and had invited Badt to visit him. Badt arrived early on the day of the visit only to find Franz still in bed. Reminiscing about the day, Badt writes that he had remained in the room with Franz while he was getting up and had teased him about how long he was taking. Franz reacted with a long disquisition on the importance of this daily awakening from the death of each night's sleep. He called it the holiest moment of the day and claimed that it should be enjoyed in every detail. He then went on to say that the luckiest persons are those who experience with full consciousness, not only this daily transition from sleep, but also the final movement from life to death, being fully conscious while taking the step from this realm to the next.[10]

Our album also contains pictures of Rosenzweig, the religious searcher. A survivor of many universities and many examinations, Rosenzweig received his doctorate in philosophy in 1912 with a brilliant dissertation on Hegel's political philosophy. But fiercer examinations were taking place in his soul, and we focus on the picture of Franz engaged in an intense conversation with a young teacher and friend, Eugen Rosenstock. The place is the University of Leipzig where Franz is taking courses in jurisprudence; the date is July 7, 1913. Rosenzweig begins the evening as a religious relativist and leaves the discussion with the decision to convert to Christianity.[11]

Shortly thereafter, Rosenstock left for Italy and Rosenzweig traveled to various cities, gathering material for his book on Hegel. He wanted to enter the Christian community as a Jew and not as a pagan and so he decided to attend the autumn high holiday services in the Reform Temple at Kassel as part of his preparation for baptism. He was there for Rosh hashana, but when his mother realized his intentions she threatened to denounce him as an apostate if he showed up on Yom Kippur. This provided a good reason for continuing his travels and thus it is that Yom Kippur 1913 found him in Berlin, where he attended services at a small Orthodox synagogue.

A turning point was reached--whether through a sudden illumination or a long churning of experience and self-knowledge.[12] He was twenty-seven when he wrote the friend he had chosen to he his godfather: ". . . I have reversed my decision. It no longer seems necessary to me, and therefore, being what I am, no longer possible. I will remain a Jew."[13]

He had earlier decided that Jesus was the way to the Father and this had been the basis of his choice to convert to Christianity. But now he writes:

> "We are wholly agreed as to what Christ and his Church mean to the world: no one can reach the Father save through him. No one can reach the Father! but the situation is quite different for one who does not have to reach the Father because he is already with him. And this is true of the people of Israel (though not of individual Jews)."[14]

Rosenzweig's decision, then, was not against Christianity. To the end of his life he maintained the conviction that Christianity is a true religion, an authentic spiritual path, but it was not to be his path. He would remain a Jew.

Other pictures follow in quick succession: Rosenzweig as an *Unteroffizier* in the Kaiser's army on the Balkan front where he began to write his monumental *Star of Redemption* on army stationery. After the war, we see him as the newlywed husband of Edith Hahn and as a teacher of Judaism, eschewing university appointments to be the director of Frankfurt's Free House of Jewish Study.[15] And shortly thereafter he appears as the proud father at the circumcision of his son, Rafael, born on September 8, 1922.

Rafael means *God Heals* and it was a custom to give that name to a boy whose parent was seriously ill when the child was born. Rosenzweig had recently received the death-sentence diagnosis of a terminal paralysis. But life did not stop. There emerged the saint and sage of Frankfurt, transforming his sickbed into study and synagogue as he continued for six years as an indefatigable scholar.

A picture to be cherished from this period is Rosenzweig hard at work translating into German the poems of Judah Halevi, a medieval master of poetry and philosophy. These have now been published as part of his *Gesammelte Schriften* and they were edited by Rafael, who was an infant when his father was producing these translations and writing commentaries on them. Writing in 1972 in the introduction to this volume of his father's work, Rafael states that the translations aimed, not merely at finding the right word for the Hebrew or Aramaic original, but at making these translations sing in the melodies familiar to German Jews.[16]

Understanding the struggle Rosenzweig engaged in with his own deteriorating health, one of the poems he translated seems particularly poignant. It is called "The Sick Doctor." It is important to remember, not only that Judah Halevi had been a doctor, but that Rosenzweig had studied medicine from 1905-1907 and had passed his preliminary examinations before transferring to the study of history and philosophy.

> Heal me and I will be whole, O my God.
> Strike me not with the fire of your angry rod.
> All cures and remedies belong solely to you,
> good or bad, strong or weak in what they do.
> You choose them with all-knowing power, not I,
> whether they strike on target or wayward fly.
> In my own remedies I place no real trust;
> from your hands alone I'll take what I must.[17]

The great scholar of Jewish mysticism, Gershom Scholem, in the reminiscences of his youth, gives us a graphic picture of Rosenzweig in those final years in the attic apartment on Schumann Street in Frankfurt. Their relationship had not been totally a happy one. Yet Scholem has no hesitation in referring to Rosenzweig as "a man of genius" and of calling the *Star* "one of the central creations of Jewish religious thought in this century." But he also characterizes the leader of the Frankfurt Lehrhaus as having "marked dictatorial inclinations;" and he admits that they differed profoundly on their understanding of German Jewishness and its future. Nevertheless, he tells us that when he was in Frankfurt in August of 1927, two years before Rosenzweig's death, he visited the paralyzed scholar for the last time. The forty-year-old Rosenzweig could no longer speak. "He could move only one finger and with it directed a specially constructed needle over an alphabet board, while his wife translated his motions into sentences. It was a heartrending visit."[18]

A final picture is not easy to forget. This time it is a real photograph, reproduced in the Nijhoff edition. I remember seeing this picture on the wall of Nahum Glatzer's study. It was taken around the time of Scholem's final visit. Rosenzweig is propped up in his bed, paralyzed, a neck support fastened to the bedstead to keep his neck from falling forward. His piercing eyes look out through rimless glasses at a world soon to be plunged into the blood-bath of World War II. What is in those eyes is inexpressible.

To the end, he was Rosenzweig the Jew, choosing life, even in the embrace of death. Martin Buber read a psalm when his forty-two-year old friend and colleague was laid to rest and someone recalled a rainbow shimmering in the distance beyond the Jewish cemetery and the silently flowing Main river. Carved large on his tombstone are the words of Psalm 73, words he chose, words addressed by the believer to his God: *ani tamid imach,* "I am always with You."

A MODERN MAN

It seemed problematic in nineteenth-century Germany that modernity and religion could have anything in common. And yet, one of the most appealing features of Franz Rosenzweig for Jew and Christian alike was his ability to be both a religious person and a modern man. The paradigm he embodies continues to provide a challenge and inspiration. The strength and soundness of his personal synthesis stand as a powerful alternative to much of the fuzziness and faltering of contemporary options.

Religion's root meaning consists of being connected with something: *religare*, to tie or anchor. In its broadest sense, religion can be understood as a connectedness with ultimacy. All religions claim that something of ultimate significance is going on in the universe and that there is a way of being connected with it. The opposite of religion in this extended sense can only be superficiality, the claim that nothing is going on except what meets the eye, what appears on the surface. Religion is a world view including more than the world.

A decision about modernity confronts all forms of religiosity. How can one be both modern and religious? What other options are there? Examining these possibilities in some detail may help to clarify the significance of Rosenzweig's thought.[19]

There is a certain logical attraction to eliminating one of the alternatives. The removal of religion to irrelevancy is perhaps the easiest course. Its popularity is undeniable. The modern Western mind-set provides a cognitive map of meanings according to which decisions are made while travelling life's road. A mild form of civil-religion is involved, occasional trips to church or synagogue, a Bible nested harmlessly on one's shelf, a perfunctory gesture towards deity on appropriate occasions.

A second benign mode of choosing modernity over religion lives mostly in academe and condescendingly reduces religion to an early effort at scientific understanding, a valuable propaedeutic to psychological awareness, or perhaps a primitive form of philosophy. The shared premise here is that religion is not explicable in terms of its own data but must be re-processed through one of the acceptable disciplines. Such an approach has no less a patron saint than Hegel.

A third form of choosing modernity over against religion has the advantage of being more straightforward and honest than the other two mentioned thus far. It may well have been most classically expressed by Ludwig Feuerbach in his Preface to *The Essence of Christianity* written in 1843:

> . . . I have sketched, with a few sharp touches, the historical solution of Christianity, and have shown that Christianity has in fact long vanished, not only from the reason but from the life of mankind, that it is nothing more than a *fixed idea*, in flagrant contradiction with our fire and life insurance companies, our railroads and steam-carriages, our picture and sculpture galleries, our military and industrial schools, our theatres and scientific museums.[20]

These words could just as easily have been written of Judaism or of any other claimant to revealed truth. Supernatural voices, smoking mountaintops, virgin births, and incarnate deities--Feuerbach relegates these to another time and place. They are images of a world which has ceased to exist, no longer meriting our attention or consideration. Freud, Marx, Nietzsche, Sartre--most great Western atheists--take Feuerbach's developed position as an obvious and unchallengeable starting point.

These first three options are ways of preferring modernity over religion. What about the reversal of this--the affirmation of religion over against modernity? This, in turn, can also take three forms: a religiosity where modernity is not even considered; a religiosity where modernity is confronted and rejected in explicit fashion; and a religiosity where modernity exists in covert form.

Certain religious societies dwell sufficiently removed from the main road of modernity that real confrontation rarely occurs. These are traditional societies into which the modern mind-set has made little or no incursion. Such people do not so much reject modernity as live in innocence of it. Such a path could in no way have been Rosenzweig's, a man who lived intensely in the modern world and mastered its methods, even passing his preliminary medical examinations before changing his major to history and eventually to philosophy.

A second form of choosing religion against modernity is both explicit and conscious. This is why Orthodox Judaism did not really exist prior to the Reform movement. Once modernity is presented as an option, then the decision to reject it becomes part of one's identity. Often this entails a self-imposed separation from the majority culture. The Essenes long ago showed the effectiveness of this method in their own rejection of Hasmonean compromise. Today one can eschew zippers and electricity with the Amish or organ transplants with ultra-observant Jews but, of course, one has to pay the price of an ideological and practical exile from modernity. This was a price which Rosenzweig nowhere shows himself prepared to pay.

A third and final way of choosing religion against modernity entails the surreptitious smuggling of the modern mind-set into the ship of faith. It is obvious that such a tack entails an inauthentic religiosity and this is precisely what characterizes much of the popular Religious Right. Here the claim is made that "old time religion" and "the plain sense of scripture" are all that are being preached, but perceptive analysts of this movement show that its real agenda includes such thoroughly modern items as nationalism and capitalism.[21]

Six options--three weighted towards modernity and three towards religion--and Rosenzweig remains free from all of them. Is there a seventh pattern? If so, how does Rosenzweig attempt it? Can he or anyone truly be both modern and religious? Perhaps the clearest way of illustrating this in summary form is to examine Rosenzweig's position on the Bible.

A MAN OF FAITH

James Collins, an outstanding historian of modern philosophy, reminded me once that it is not given to us to live without biases; our only human option is to be aware of them. Modernity is a bias and Rosenzweig was modern. But in his case it was a bias of which he had a sharp awareness. Interestingly, the clearest indication that one knows one's bias is the ability to identify it as a perspective. Correspondingly, the greatest danger of every bias consists precisely in its not being recognized as a perspective, but as the way things really are.

Rosenzweig was not free of biases, whether as a modern man, as a Jew, or as a German. But he had a clear awareness that his perspectives were indeed perspectives. Although capable of processing knowledge through those methodologies legitimated by the modern mind-set, he was able to exist and know outside of their limitations. Although a Jew, he was able to ascribe truth to non-Jewish religiosity. Although a German, he escaped the lure of that atavistic fundamentalism of race and blood which led to his country's devastation.

Nowhere can Rosenzweig's simultaneous *use of* and *freedom from* modernity better be seen than in his writings about the Bible. I know of no better touchstone for determining how people relate religion and modernity than in the way they read the Bible. The six options sketched above regarding the relationship of religion and modernity all generate a correlate position on the Bible. Rosenzweig's view on the Bible shows us the genius and carefulness of his seventh way.

The traditional Jewish community, except for an occasional freethinker like Spinoza, had by and large accepted as a fact that God had dictated the Torah to Moses in Hebrew. German "higher criticism" (named after the kind of textual study which went beyond merely establishing a critical edition of a classic work) had found evidence for different strata of tradition in the texts of the Bible and thus had exposed the Bible as an edited work. This kind of scholarship shattered the earlier belief about the nature of biblical inspiration and the consequent integrity of the text for most of the educated world and, in the process, had destroyed the faith of many Jews.

Rosenzweig adhered to a *via media*, neither denying the legitimate directions of current scholarship nor abandoning his faith. Here we see his character-istic stance of being both a modern man, trained in the canons of the German university system, and a man of faith, formed by deep religious experience. The Reform movement accepted the conclusions of modern biblical scholarship, but often lost the transcendent dimension of the biblical literature, reducing it finally to a perceptive ethical code. Orthodox Jewry, on the other hand, maintained its faith by denying the validity of biblical criticism and adhering to the traditional view of biblical inspiration.

In expressing his dissatisfaction with both the orthodox and the extreme liberal position, Rosenzweig wrote in 1927:

> Our difference from orthodox Judaism lies in the fact that our belief in the holiness (and therefore the privileged position) of the Torah and its revelational character does not lead us to draw any conclusions about the stages in which the

text was developed or about the text's philosophical worth. Our faith is not the least bit disturbed if Wellhausen is right in all his theories and if the Samaritans really do have the better text of the Torah."[22]

Rosenzweig goes on to say that although he cannot believe with Orthodox Jews that Moses himself was the author of the whole Torah, he differs from the liberal higher critics in understanding the Letter *R*, not as the scholar's abbreviation for "redactor" or editor of the text, but as *rabbenu*, i.e., our teacher, Moses, and all those sages within the Jewish community responsible for the development of the text through the thousand-year period in which the books of the Hebrew Bible were assembled.[23] This example is paradigmatic of Rosenzweig's unique ability to employ the secular scholars' valid research methodologies without following them in their various faith-eliminating reductionisms.

Rosenzweig is the prototype of the modern man of faith, living between the alternatives of an absolute unchanging belief and a dogmatically closed unbelief. He once wrote:

> Modern man is neither a believer nor an unbeliever. He believes and he doubts. And so he is nothing, but he is alive. Belief and unbelief 'happen' to him and all that he is required to do is not run away from what is happening but make use of it once it has happened. This seems very simple when one has not entered the field of action, but it is actually so difficult that there is probably no one who has managed it on more than a very few, rare occasions.[24]

This is what ultimately characterizes Rosenzweig's
thought, the honest embracing of a process including
both belief and unbelief.

Rosenzweig's mature life was spent close to the
text of the Bible. At the time of his death, he was
collaborating with Martin Buber on the monumental
task of translating the Hebrew Bible into German. One
has only to read through the two volumes of his *Briefe
und Tagebücher* to see the extraordinary attention
given to the Bible: detailed textual questions, problems
of translation, and methods of studying the biblical
texts. Rosenzweig's immense enthusiasm for the Bible
is everywhere transparent.

Just a few months before he experiences the first
symptoms of his fatal paralysis, Rosenzweig writes to
Rabbi Benno Jacob:

> It is late in the evening and I have
> just finished reading with breathless
> excitement your *Critique of Sources and
> Exegesis* which I found yesterday afternoon
> in a bookstore. I am totally fascinated by
> the book. I am myself something of an
> old philologist and I have real feeling for
> the kind of presentation you make, built
> up from countless little bits of stone.
> Someday I hope to see a commentary by
> you on the whole Torah. You would be
> the man for it![25]

Rosenzweig's enthusiasm is sincere but more important
for our purposes is what follows--the delineation of that
careful working together of the old and the new, seeking a faithfulness that is modern and a modernity that
is faithful:

> One feels in almost everything you
> say the pulse of Judaism's spiritual
> history. You have so much more than the
> little discoveries of the past which modern

commentaries never give us any respite from and which actually prevent people from seeing what stares them in the face in the text. You do a beautiful job of freeing the reader from those dangers.[26]

What we see here is the use of modern scholarship not to erode faith but to facilitate its growth in the context of modernity.

Both extremes of the religious spectrum seem endangered by the confusion of factuality and religious truth. What the liberals love to deny, the traditionalists seem bound to defend. But Rosenzweig steers through this Scylla and Charybdis, seeking always a dialogical faith. We see this in a letter he writes to Hans Ehrenberg on January 29, 1925:

> As far as miracles go--I really try to avoid them. Perhaps it's possible for me to believe in every miracle but I don't care to. I don't want to overburden myself. All those prophecies in Isaiah about Hezekiah's contemporaries I could only believe if that faith really paid off. I only want to believe where I am constrained to believe or where it comes to me completely on its own. So I do not even believe in the miracle of the Red Sea or of Sinai as much as I believe the whole thing. It is my strong conviction that miracles are a part of all of this but the ones reported in the Bible might be wrongly reported; maybe the real miracles are even more marvelous. In any case, all writings are poison, even holy writings. They only suit my taste when they're translated back into spoken language.[27]

Even scripture must become dialogue again, real address and response, in order to be true. The Bible is not so much revelation as the written word which comes from revelatory experience and which, through the encounter with a faithful person, can become again the living, revelatory disclosure.

In an essay on Luther's translation of the Bible, Rosenzweig writes:

> As a searchlight detaches from darkness now one section of the landscape and now another, and then leaves these again dimmed, so for such a man the days of his own life illumine the Scriptures, and in their quality of humanness permit him to recognize what is more than human, today at one point and tomorrow at another, nor can one day ever vouch for the next to yield a like experience. . . . This humanness may anywhere become so translucid under the beam of a day of one's life, that it stands suddenly written in his innermost heart; and to him for that one pulse beat it is as if--at that instant--he heard a voice calling to his heart. Not everything in the Scriptures belongs to him--neither today nor ever. But he knows that he belongs to everything in them, and it is only this readiness of his which, when it is directed toward the Scriptures, constitutes belief.[28]

This approach to scripture has all the passion of religion which distinguishes it from the lukewarm liberalism which Rosenzweig all too often encountered. But it is no less distinct from the literalism which plagues religious reactionaries whose passion seems to be not so much for God as against modern scholarship.

Rosenzweig's position was one in which there was no fear, neither fear of the tradition with its demand for commitment nor fear of modernity with its insistence on rational methodology. He hears the call of the former, even in his modern life. And he respects the canons of the latter, even with its intrinsic inability to calculate transcendence.

This, then, becomes the essential project of Jewish faithfulness. Not the choice of total fulfillment of the 613 commandments or total avoidance of them. The "love it or leave it" policy shows itself to be as simplistic in faith as it is in politics. Religious reality must be the experiencing today of the inner power of the divine. And, therefore, it is not a matter of doing everything but of doing something where that something can be real.

> "Therefore, whether much is done, or little, or maybe nothing at all, is immaterial in the face of the one and unavoidable demand, that whatever is being done, shall come from that inner power. As the knowledge of everything knowable is not yet wisdom, so the doing of everything do-able is not yet deed. The deed is created at the boundary of the merely do-able, where the voice of commandment causes the spark to leap from 'I must' to 'I can.'"[29]

Rosenzweig's analogy is telling. The gap between knowledge and wisdom is not less than that between mere religious observance and true spirituality.

And yet, just as stored information can open the door to wisdom, so the wealth of Jewish observance can be the beginning of faithful living. The Jew seeking spiritual growth must choose something she can do, something flowing from her reality--lighting Sabbath candles, studying Torah, praying the Psalms. It is not the quantity of do-able things which is significant but the quality of expectation and readiness. The beginning of faithfulness lies in doing whatever is at hand to do, but with a readiness for meeting God.

Every moment contains the possibility of encountering the divine. Isn't that what Martin Buber means about his own sense of religion?

> "I have given up the 'religious' which is nothing but the exception, extraction, exaltation, ecstasy; or it has given me up. I possess nothing but the everyday out of which I am never taken. The Mystery is no longer disclosed, it has escaped or it has made its dwelling here where everything happens as it happens. . . . I do not know much more. If that is religion then it is just *everything*, simply all that is lived in its possibility of dialogue."[30]

Reality's ultimate presence may break through in any moment of any day. The beginning of faithfulness is attentiveness. As Rosenzweig himself wrote, "The highest things cannot be planned; for them, readiness is everything."[31]

It is precisely this readiness which differentiates Rosenzweig's position from the kind of liberal theologizing which finally bogs down in a mire of merely interesting opinions and from the reactionary fundamentalism which can all too readily defend itself against modernity only to lose its capacity for radical response and service in the world. Rosenzweig's greatness lies in his unique ability to be a modern man and a man of faith. Rabbi Abraham Joshua Heschel often stressed the necessity of inter-faith dialogue being grounded in faith. It is indeed as a man of faith that Rosenzweig becomes a bridge to new possibilities of Jewish-Christian dialogue, for he takes us beyond the polemics of traditionalism versus liberalism with their respective rejection of either modernity or faith to a common ground which can encompass both.

CHAPTER ONE

NOTES

1. From Franz Rosenzweig, *Briefe und Tagebücher*, I-1 (The Hague: Martinus Nijhoff Publishers, 1979), p. 287. Translation my own.

2. From Casper's introductory essay: Rosenzweig, *Briefe und Tagebücher*, I-1, xiv.   Translation my own; the emphasis is in the original.

3. Rosenzweig, *Briefe und Tagebücher*, I-1, p. 1036. Translation my own.

4. Rosenzweig, *Briefe und Tagebücher*, I-1, p. 7. Translation my own.   The original is a ten-line poem written in rhyming couplets.   The first line (Lieber Gott, der Du bist auf Erden) is an obvious play on the opening of the Lord's Prayer, "Vater unser, der Du bist im Himmel."   Thus I kept the archaic English still used in the Lord's Prayer.

5. The city was first mentioned in historical records in 913 and celebrated its millennium of existence in 1913, a year of monumental significance in Rosenzweig's personal history.

6. This story was told to me by Nahum Glatzer as a personal reminiscence shared with him by Rosenzweig, when they were together in Frankfurt.

7. Rosenzweig, *Briefe und Tagebücher*, I-2, p. 1143. Translation my own.

8. "But Israel stretched out his right hand and laid it on Ephraim's head, though he was the younger, and his left hand on Manasseh's head--thus crossing his hands--although Manasseh was the

first-born." Genesis 48:14 in the Jewish Publication Society translation. This translation will be used for all subsequent quotations from the Hebrew Bible.

9. Rosenzweig, *Briefe und Tagebücher*, I-1, p. 15. The translation is by Nahum N. Glatzer and can be found on p. 3 of his excellent introductory work, *Franz Rosenzweig: His Life and Thought* (New York: Schocken Books, 1961).

10. This story by Hermann Badt is found after the text of Rosenzweig's invitation letter in Rosenzweig, *Briefe und Tagebücher*, I-1, p. 85.

11. Rivka Horwitz has written an interesting article on this phase of Rosenzweig's life. It is entitled "Judaism Despite Christianity," and is in vol. 24, #3 (summer 1975) of *Judaism*, pp. 306-318.

12. There are two viewpoints on this. Glatzer (p. xviii in the introduction to *Franz Rosenzweig: His Life and Thought*), basing his view on communications with Rosenzweig's mother, understands the Yom Kippur event as a sudden illumination. Rosenzweig's wife, with whom I spoke in Berlin in March of 1976, saw the whole process as a gradual one. Given the interplay of conscious and unconscious movements in any major decision, both views may be correct from differing perspectives. For a fuller description of Nahum Glatzer's perspective on this event, see his essay, "Franz Rosenzweig: The Story of a Conversion" in his *Essays on Jewish Thought* (Alabama: University of Alabama Press, 1978), pp. 230-242.

13. Glatzer. *Franz Rosenzweig: His Life and Thought*, p. 28.

14. Glatzer. *Franz Rosenzweig: His Life and Thought*, p. 341.

15. For a further description of the Lehrhaus, see Nahum Glatzer's essay, "The Frankfort Lehrhaus" in his *Essays on Jewish Thought* (University AL: The University of Alabama Press, 1978), pp. 254-273.

16. From Franz Rosenzweig, *Sprachdenken im Übersetzen*, Book Four of the *Gesammelte Schriften*, volume one: *Hymnen und Gedichte des Jehuda Halevi* (The Hague: Martinus Nijhoff Publishers, 1983) p. xi.

17. This is my own free translation of Rosenzweig's German, *Sprachdenken im Ubersetzen*, p. 126. There seems to be a misprint in the Nijhoff edition of the poem and I am reading the word *Ziel* for the word *Zeil* which is in the text.

18. The quotations in this paragraph are all from Gershom Scholem's *From Berlin to Jerusalem*, translated from the German by Harry Zohn (New York: Schocken Books, 1980), pp. 139-141.

19. For further treatment of the relationship of Judaism to modernity, see Emil L. Fackenheim's book, *What is Judaism? An Interpretation For the Present Age*, (New York: Summit Books, 1987), especially pages 22-29.

20. Ludwig Feuerbach, *The Essence of Christianity*, trans. by George Elliot (New York: Harper, 1957), p. xliv.

21. See, for example, the perceptive analysis contained in Gabriel Fackre, *The Religious Right & Christian Faith* (Grand Rapids, Michigan: Wm. B. Eerdmans Publishing Co., 1982). Also helpful in this area are

God, Reason, and the Evangelicals by Nicholas F. Gier (Lanham, MD: University Press of America, 1987) and *Redemptorama* by Carol Flake (Anderson Press, Doubleday and Company, 1984).

22. Rosenzweig, *Briefe und Tagebücher*, I-2, p. 1134. Translation my own. Julius Wellhausen was one of the pioneer higher critics. His *History of Israel* (1878) made a profound and lasting impression on biblical scholarship.

23. Rosenzweig, *Briefe und Tagebücher*, I-2, p. 1134.

24. Glatzer. *Franz Rosenzweig: His Life and Thought*, p. 258.

25. Rosenzweig, *Briefe und Tagebücher*, I-2, p. 706. Translation my own.

26. Rosenzweig, *Briefe und Tagebücher*, I-2, p. 706. Translation my own.

27. Rosenzweig, *Briefe und Tagebücher*, I-2, p. 1022. Translation my own.

28. Glatzer. *Franz Rosenzweig: His Life and Thought*, p. 258.

29. Franz Rosenzweig, *On Jewish Learning*, ed. N. N. Glatzer (New York: Schocken Press, 1965), p. 86.

30. Martin Buber, *Between Man and Man*, trans. Ronald Gregor Smith (New York: McMillan Press, 1966), p. 14.

31. Rosenzweig, *On Jewish Learning*, p. 65.

EARLY WRITINGS

THE QUESTION ABOUT REVELATION

The consideration of Rosenzweig's relationship to the Bible brings us ineluctably to the larger issue of revelation. This will be our focus in these next two chapters, both because it is so central in the development of Rosenzweig's thought and because it is the crucial theological source of a new paradigm for understanding Judaism and Christianity, both in themselves and in their relationship to each other.

Emerging from a forest of evergreens in the Harz mountains, Franz Rosenzweig asked Rudolf Ehrenberg a question; this question was to become the leitmotif of Rosenzweig's theology of revelation. Three years later he reminds his cousin of that day in 1914 when he had asked him whether it was possible (and if so, how), by any purely philosophical or generally demonstrable criteria, to distinguish revelation from all properly human forms of knowledge.[1] He was twenty-eight years old when he asked that question and before he reached the age of forty-three Franz Rosenzweig was dead, but in those few years he made an invaluable contribution to the modern understanding of revelation.

In some senses, this question was never answered--not because it was too difficult a question, but because it was the wrong question. It had been framed as an epistemological question, a knowledge question. How is the kind of knowledge which is revelation different from other kinds of knowledge, and how can this difference be established? The underlying premise seems to be that revelation is indeed a form of knowledge, i.e., the

propositional knowledge which dominated the philoso-
phies and theologies of Germany in 1914. But
Rosenzweig's own thought and experience were already
moving him away from the assumptions about revelation which had been shared by generations of theologians.

Revelation is not a common word in the Hebrew
Bible. We read that God "came down upon Mount
Sinai" (Exodus 19:20) and later that "the Lord would
speak to Moses face to face, as one man speaks to
another" (Exodus 33:11)--typically, these are the more
concrete kinds of expressions which characterize
Hebrew thought. Revelation has a Greek heritage and
it is in the course of dialogue with Hellenistic thought
that Jewish thinkers came to expound on revelation.
Thus, while we do not expect to find a treatise on
revelation in the Hebrew Bible, we are not surprised to
find the topic addressed in the writings of Saadia, the
10th century Gaon or spiritual leader of the talmudic
academy of Sura in Babylonia. Saadia encountered
Greek thought as mediated through the Arab writers
and his *magnum opus, Beliefs and Opinions,* is
generally acknowledged as the first systematic
presentation of Judaism as a rational body of beliefs.[2]

Saadia treats revelation in his discussion of
knowledge; there are three ordinary sources of
knowledge: direct observation, intellectual intuition, and
logical inference.[3] There is a fourth source for "the
community of monotheists" and that additional source
of knowledge is authentic tradition.[4] Revelation, as the
basis of authentic tradition, facilitates the entire flow of
knowledge; reasoning to important truths requires
training, time, and skill. By means of revelation,
"women and young people and those who have no
aptitude for speculation can have a perfect and
accessible faith."[5] Since the ordinary person operates
most comfortably on the level of sense knowledge, God
sent the divine messengers and prophets so that people
could see the signs and miracles, and from observation,
grow to obedience.[6]

Some two hundred years after Saadia, Moses Maimonides stressed the exactness and specificity of the content of revelation, stating that "the whole of the law was written by Moses our Teacher before his death in his own hand."[7] This refers to Torah in its strict sense, the first five books of the Hebrew Bible. But Maimonides also asserts that:

> although the oral Law was not committed to writing, Moses taught the whole of it, in his court, to the seventy elders as well as to Eleazar, Phineas, and Joshua--all three of whom received it from Moses."[8]

Here there is no doubt that revelation has content and that the content is knowledge.

And so it seems that Rosenzweig's question in 1914 had long been answered by the Jewish philosophical tradition. The content of revelation was received through the senses--a voice was heard, signs were seen, words were written--but because these elements of voice, signs, and written words came from God, the whole process is manifestly different from ordinary knowledge and thus is properly understood as divine revelation.

Rosenzweig's question, of course, could not be answered so simply because he was not only a Jew, like Saadia and Mainonides, but a modern man. Can a modern man believe, for example, that a voice was heard on Sinai articulating words in Hebrew which a tape-recorder could have preserved for our ears today? This was a pre-modern assumption shared by Jews and Christians alike who believed in the veracity of the revelation given to Moses. Jewish philosophers had long been troubled with this empirical basis of faith, but not to the point of denying it. Philo of Alexandria, a Jewish philosopher contemporary with the beginnings of Christianity, had long ago stated his theory:

The ten words or oracles, in reality laws or statutes, were delivered by the Father of All when the nation, men and women alike, were assembled together. Did he do so by His own utterance in the form of a voice? Surely not: may no such thought ever enter our minds, for God is not a man needing a mouth and tongue and windpipe. I should suppose that God wrought on this occasion a miracle of a truly holy kind by bidding an invisible sound to be created in the air more marvelous than all instruments and fitted with perfect harmonies, not soulless, nor yet composed of body and soul like a living creature, but a rational soul full of clearness and distinctness, which giving shape and tension to the air and changing it to flaming fire, sounded forth like a breath through a trumpet an articulate voice so loud that it appeared to be equally audible to the farthest as well as the nearest.[9]

However he embellishes on the kind of voice involved, Philo is asserting a knowledge content communicated through an audible voice.

Judah Halevi, a 12th-century Jewish poet and philosopher much less enamored of reason than Philo, Saadia, or Maimonides, writes:

We say, then, that we do not know how the intention became corporealised and the speech evolved which struck our ear, nor what new thing God created from nought, nor what existing thing He employed, for he does not lack the power. . . . As the water stood at His command, shaped itself at His will, so the air which touched the prophet's ear, assumed the form of sounds, which conveyed these matters to be communicated by God to the prophet and the people.[10]

Halevi remains in the tradition insofar as he understands revelation as a knowledge content, communicated by God, in an extraordinary but sense perceptible way. Some seven hundred years after Halevi's *Kuzari*, S. L. Steinheim defended the thesis that revelation, understood as a particular knowledge content, is of such a character that it can reach man only through the ear by an audible word from outside.[11] This understanding of revelation is shared by many Jews and Christians to this day, but it was not shared by Franz Rosenzweig.

Something more than modernity and the tradition of higher criticism was behind Rosenzweig's development of a nonconceptual theology of revelation. Our focus here will be on something of Rosenzweig's early background and writings: his relationship to Eugen Rosenstock, the important but only obliquely acknowledged experience of Yom Kippur 1913, the essay entitled "Atheistic Theology" written in April 1914, his correspondence with Rosenstock in 1916, and his letters of 1917, especially the very important one written to Rudolf Ehrenberg.

It may not be a meaningless coincidence that a deep passion for music characterized so many of the thinkers we call "existentialists." In the case of Rosenzweig, his love of music seems to have been a propaedeutic for an awareness of religious reality as irreducible to the rational moments it contains. We already sensed part of this horizon of Rosenzweig's thought when we heard him at the age of nineteen, wishing that he were a Beethoven symphony or something already completed.[12] He longs to be finished, written, fully composed, and yet he is already aware that life is the process of being written, being composed.

He admits to being a romantic. He writes in 1908, on his return to Freiburg, that he had come there in his first year as a hopeless romantic and had left at the end of that year as the driest of scholars, but he goes on to say that he returns now neither the one nor the other, but both.[13]   Writing to his parents when he was twenty, Rosenzweig describes a visit to a museum in Venice and the impression made by a picture there:

> And you sit there a few minutes on the rococo chair and then a miracle happens which causes all the details which I have been describing to disappear and one sees without knowing what one sees; one becomes total seeing, without any passion, without any excitement, without any thoughts, without any knowledge of something else or of oneself: total seeing. That is absolute art, just as you can speak of absolute music--music that does not describe anything (most music is secretly program music, even when it does not call itself that) but it is only music and it can only be *heard*. That is something so incomprehensible that it could be the foundation of a religion.[14]

Absolute art where we see but do not know; absolute music where we hear but do not see--these are presented as incomprehensible phenomena, analogous to the originating experiences of a religious tradition. The analogy is compelling. If there is an artistic experience in which a person becomes only seeing, and an experience of pure music which renders a person only hearing, then what are the founding experiences of a religion or the purest moments within a religious tradition? We would hardly expect them to be conceptualizable, since mere knowing was left behind even in the aesthetic experience. Almost imperceptibly, a door is being opened in Rosenzweig's life which will give easier access to a future still hidden from him in 1906.

"ATHEISTIC THEOLOGY"

One of the most significant ideas that Rosenstock communicated to Rosenzweig during their seminal conversation in Leipzig on July 7, 1913 was an understanding of revelation as orientation; after the experience and event of revelation, there is a real "above and below" and "before and after" in the flow of human events. The center of things is no longer simply the place where an individual happens to be standing. There is an objective point of orientation, the place where God enters history, and any individual life can be authentic only with reference to this.[15] Three months later, in the 1913 Yom Kippur experience, Rosenzweig realized this sense of orientation in his own Jewishness.

What is most germane to our investigation at this point is the fact that revelation now emerges as the key to Rosenzweig's thought; the restoral of revelation to its proper place within theology becomes Rosenzweig's self-appointed task.[16] There is clear evidence of this newly emergent Rosenzweig in the essay which he wrote in 1914 entitled "Atheistic Theology."[17] This significant essay remains somehow a neglected child of Rosenzweig's thought. The volume Martin Buber had invited him to write it for was never published; it is barely alluded to in Glatzer's basic introduction to Rosenzweig, and seventy years after being penned, it remains largely unknown to the English-speaking public.[18] And yet, it was this essay which Rosenzweig read to Rudolf Ehrenberg on their walk through the Harz mountains in 1914, the time when Rosenzweig formulated the question with which we began our investigation, a time still proximate to his Yom Kippur experience; it was his first essay on Jewish religious thought, the first sustained effort to formulate his understanding of revelation. It was this insight into revelation which gave Rosenzweig his "long-sought Archimedes-point"[19]--the position from which he could and did move the theological world.

To grasp the significance of this early literary product of Rosenzweig's religious thought, it is necessary to make some reference to the impact of Hegelianism on the German philosophical and theological world, as well as to an emerging opposition to the hegemony of Hegel's thought. Rosenstock once referred to Rosenzweig as "a Jew after Christ's birth and Hegel's death."[20] The phrase gives us a thumbnail sketch of Rosenzweig's personal and intellectual world, resting on the three pillars of Judaism, Hegel's philosophy, and Christianity. Rosenzweig's relationship to the latter two elements was multi-valent; in one sense, his identity makes no ultimate sense without the religion of Christ and the philosophy of Hegel. Christianity was a positive influence in Rosenzweig's conversion to Judaism, just as Hegelianism was an important moment in the development of Rosenzweig's existentialism. While he remained indebted both to Christianity and Hegelianism, his own religious and philosophical identity constituted him as a minority of one standing against these twin Goliaths.

We have already seen the unprecedented religious career of an assimilated Jew moving back to his Judaism via a profound personal encounter with Christianity. No less surprising is his development of a personal philosophy of dialogue after his total immersion into Hegel's Idealism. In this, Rosenzweig was not without predecessors, though their number was not large. They were much like the tiny band of sixteenth-century navigators, those thinkers of the late nineteenth century who shoved off from the shores of Idealism and sailed out bravely on an uncharted sea. They had no assurance that they would ever reach another shore, or even if there was another shore to reach. Had Kierkegaard, "that grim and grisly monster without confession and so without Church,"[21] found another shore before his body collapsed in the streets of Copenhagen? What new land had Nietzsche failed to reach when his mind was set adrift on the shoreless sea of insanity a full ten years before his death? These precedents gave small hope of anyone faring better.

But it was despite this danger that Rosenzweig did choose to sail out beyond the known shores of Idealism. The stifling fullness of Hegel's world left him with an intense longing for *Lebensraum*, space for his unique life experience. Hegel's world encroached on everything; it was all-encompassing. In the famous letter which contains the embryo of his *magnum opus*, Rosenzweig writes:

> Naive metaphysics teaches that the earth rests on a great elephant and the great elephant on a great turtle and so on *ad infinitum*. Hegel teaches that the earth rests on a great snake and the great snake holds itself up by biting its own tail. Consequently, Hegel can indeed give an exhaustive clarification of the earth-snake system, but he does not make it at all clear why the entire system fails to collapse. My explanation is that it neither falls nor moves because there is no room for either--no "where to" for falling and no "where in" for moving. The snake fills all possible space; the snake is every bit as massive as the earth which rests on it.[22]

Hegel's system filled everything; nothing seemed left over. Rosenzweig's basic project becomes clear. Space had to be won, breathing space for God, humanity, and the world. There must be a distance before there can be relating. And this is why nineteenth-century Idealism, by dissolving all differences into an ultimate identity, removed the basis for any real mutuality. When two banks of a river are said to be really one, not only are the distinct banks being denied, but the possibility of building a bridge is *a fortiori* also negated. In order for there to be even the possibility of revelation, there must be at least two distinct entities: God and a human being. Some could accept a medieval world picture in which humankind paled into insignificance before the mystery and authority of God; others could follow Feuerbach in reducing God to the collective projection of humanity's ideals, an alienated mirror image of the human community. But Rosenzweig consistently emerges as the thinker who insists on a world in relationship to both God and human beings. He will claim all the new gains for human subjectivity in the postmedieval world, but he will not, and really he cannot, dismiss the mystery of God by any kind of facile reductionism. He walks a precarious middle path and we are already made aware of this in his 1914 essay, "Atheistic Theology."

The paradox of the title seems to anticipate the "death-of-God-theology" and "religionless Christianity" which became current in theology several decades later. For Rosenzweig, a theology is atheistic when it attempts to live simplistically without the tension entailed by recognizing both its divine and human poles. He sees the theologies which surround him--both Christian and Jewish--as working in a Hegelian context in which God has been totally reduced to an immanent factor of human evolution. In other words, Jesus is no longer seen as a divine-human paradox, the revelation of God in flesh; he is rather an ideal human being. And the Jewish people are no longer viewed as the particularist-universalist paradox of a chosen people, the space- and time-bound locus of the design, will, and love of a God not bound by space and time; Jews are now an ideal human community, a group precocious in its moral evolution.[23]

For Rosenzweig, these developments bring both Judaism and Christianity perilously close to a Feuerbachian type of atheism. Instead of understanding the human over against the power and mystery of the divine, these Hegelian theologies settle for viewing the divine as the self-projection of the human against the heaven of myth.[24] And myth is something which Rosenzweig understands as living from its own light, not needing God's light.[25] The current theologies were caught by an operative reductionism whereby the initiative-taking God's breaking into the house of humanity is turned around to an inner-human dialectic, i.e., the incarnation becomes the humanness of the god-idea and the descent to Sinai becomes the autonomy of the ethical law. This involves an ultimate identification of the kingdom of God with the human project, a change profoundly affecting both Judaism and Christianity; the whole transcendent referent is displaced, along with the orientational context of revelation alluded to earlier, the before and after constituted by life between creation and final divine fulfillment.[26]

All the language is saved, but Rosenzweig maintains that the whole reality has disappeared. This is the real significance of theology becoming atheistic. Since God is our self-projection, revelation becomes the mythical statement of the human community's dialectical relationship with itself. Rosenzweig sets forth his central view here:

What seems to be set aside is precisely the distinctiveness of God and the human person, the frightening scandal for every kind of paganism, both ancient and modern. Thus the crucial factor in revelation is brought to silence--namely, the very content of divinity plunging into the unworthy human vessel.[27]

Rosenzweig takes his stand here with the sharpness of the Kierkegaardian either-or. Either there is a real distinction between God and humanity, with the consequent possibility of a bridge between them being built, or everything is explicable in terms of our human experience, and revelation consequently translates into myth. Rosenzweig opts for revelation as real event.

The language employed by Rosenzweig to describe revelation in this early essay seems very Barthian. God's entry into the human community is *hereinbrechen* and *hereinstürzen*, a breaking-into or plunging-into a seemingly passive human recipient.[28] Just as Rosenzweig would later find Rosenstock's idea of revelation as orientation true but inadequate so, too, he was to find this head-on-encounter model of revelation too limited. By the time he is really on the path of his fully developed thought, when he writes the *Urzelle* or "germ-cell" of *The Star* in 1917, Rosenzweig has moved beyond both of these earlier steps to a dialogical model.

Before leaving this collision model of revelation, it would seem appropriate to be aware of the insight this gives us into Rosenzweig's Yom Kippur experience of 1913; there he possibly encountered God in a way that called for an about-face in his own plans and life directions. He was moved from an imminent baptism with his accompanying confession of Jesus as the way to the Father to an awareness that his life as a Jew was already with the Father and required no mediatorship.[29]

In denying the reductionistic move in either of its directions--namely, dissolving the human into the divine or the divine into the human--Rosenzweig writes:

> If this half, the human person, were simply in himself and without inner contradiction, then a thinker, just as much as any business-person, could indeed dispense with God.[30]

In other words, the human mystery is not adequately understood without this transcendent referent, which Rosenzweig sees here primarily as a kind of inner contradiction. Now this can in no way be construed as a proof. The very idea of proving something entails establishing it in terms of something prior which is true; proofs, therefore, are *apriori* impossible for primary reality experiences.

While not a proof, this kind of statement points to the kind of experience which validates Rosenzweig's basic schema. The continuing argument against the adequacy of "secular humanity," i.e., the human person without a transcendent context, is based on reflection upon the transcendent nature of the horizons of human experience. Just as animals cannot be adequately understood within the limitations of plant categories, humans cannot make sense out of the borders of their experience without a connection with transcendence. No truth exists for us completely outside our own skin; we can, nevertheless, believe that this skin, unlike Hegel's snake or fresco, is not identical with the parameters of all that is.

LETTERS TO ROSENSTOCK

The year 1916 represents a further development in Rosenzweig's theology of revelation; this is evidenced primarily in the letters exchanged between Rosenzweig and Rosenstock during this year. On December 24, 1916--the day before his thirtieth birthday--Rosenzweig writes to Rudolf Ehrenberg, "The real experience and achievement of these last months for me is my exchange of letters with Rosenstock."[31] The correspondence had been initiated with Rosenstock's letter of May 29, 1916. He had a few weeks' furlough from the Verdun front and wrote the letter from the Rosenzweig family home in Kassel; Rosenzweig was far from his home then, serving in the German army on the Macedonian front.[32]

In an autobiographical work written almost forty years after Rosenzweig's death, Rosenstock refers to his friend and former student, Franz Rosenzweig, and specifically to the letters they sent back and forth between the eastern and western fronts of the German army in 1916. He writes about the effect the exchange had on both of them, especially what he discerns as an exchange of life rhythm. Rosenstock had an early burst of energy and had completed his doctorate and begun teaching at twenty-four; Rosenzweig sat in his classroom at the age of twenty-eight, a man still looking for the direction of his life. But then, between

1918 and 1919, Rosenzweig had written his major work and begun a course of incredible productivity which continued, only hindered not halted by his nine-year illness, until his early death. As Rosenstock expresses this:

> Eugen learns final patience and Franz finally becomes impatient. Like the ivory balls in a billiard game in their exchange of impact, so did those life rhythms exchange their force, Franz to Eugen, Eugen to Franz. The insight into this exchange seems the most important fact about this correspondence and, to me at least, is even more important than the admittedly significant content of the letters. For we still know so very little about human life rhythms.[33]

Rosenzweig, the late starter, was now ready to erupt into activity.

Important steps along Rosenzweig's path form a clearer pattern now: his abandonment of relativism after his talk with Rosenstock on July 7, 1913; his decision to remain a Jew after a chain of events culminating in the Yom Kippur experience of October 11, 1913; his 1914 essay on "Atheistic Theology;" and now this correspondence, another step along the way. In 1916 Rosenzweig refers to revelation as "that great victorious breaking in of spirit into what is not spirit. . ."[34] And then, in the same letter, he goes on to ask of Rosenstock, ". . .explain to me your present idea of the relation between nature and revelation."[35]

Rosenzweig's capsule characterization of revelation contains as many problems as answers. His use of the phrase "breaking in" shows his maintenance here of the collision model of revelation found in "Atheistic Theology." But what is meant in calling this event "victorious?" And how can one believe in creation and yet speak of the recipient of revelation as "what is not spirit"?

Rosenstock's response indicates a dissatisfaction with Rosenzweig's way of posing the problem; it is not nature and revelation which are comparable but natural understanding and revelation.[36] Natural understanding entails the relativistic, self-oriented stance which characterized Rosenzweig's earlier life and was the subject of his talk with Rosenstock on July 7, 1913. Revelation is made possible only by the abandonment of the ego-defined space where one can be the center of the universe.[37] But how can this position be abandoned without disintegration and self-destruction? This is where Rosenstock's faith in Jesus as the incarnate Logos comes into play; the Logos is not caught in the net of relativism, of only being able to measure itself by itself. And so when the Word becomes flesh in Jesus, this same absolute orientation comes into history. The Christian revelation is the healing of the Babel of confused tongues, which is the necessary consequence of mere natural understanding; it is now worthwhile to think and speak again because thought, too, as well as speech and life itself, has a standard outside itself, the Word made flesh.[38]

Two days later, on October 30, Rosenstock writes again to Rosenzweig and continues his reflections on revelation. "All revelation is something that gives us a standard, and at the same time it is a sensible, perceptible event. . . ."[39] This further clarifies the pivotal importance which the Christian doctrine of Incarnation has in Rosenstock's theology of revelation. For there in the sensible, perceptible reality of Jesus, faith simultaneously encounters the Word of God.

This is a crucial point in the correspondence. It almost seems that Rosenzweig had been drawing Rosenstock out, encouraging him to play his hand openly, to create some real space for serious dialogue. Rosenzweig's letter of November 7 brings the whole history of Jewish-Christian dialogue to a new level of self-understanding, but our concern here is only with its relevance to the subject of revelation. Rosenzweig approves of the translation of Isaiah 7:9 as: "If you do

not believe, you do not abide."[40]   He concurs with
Rosenstock's recognition of a connection with something
absolute as part of revelation. Revealing is the action
named from the side of God's initiative-taking; believing
is the same reality from the side of the human partner;
and abiding is the resulting ensoulled speech and newly
empowered fire, i.e., life freed from the ego-prison of
relativism.

    This idea of revelation as absolute orientation
appears in other parts of this correspondence of 1916.
In a letter of November 30, Rosenzweig mentions in an
almost casual way that the essence of revelation is to
bring an absolute symbolic ordering to history.[41]   It is
clear that for him, this is what distinguishes Judaism
and Christianity from all forms of pagan and natural
religiosity. In an undated letter, Rosenzweig states
explicitly that the common ground shared by Judaism
and Christianity is the human aspect of the common
objective origin of revelation.[42]   And this allows these
two religions to be otherworldly, while breathing the
world with every breath.[43]   In other words, they live
from this crossroads, this juncture of God with human
history, the Absolute with the relative.

    There is one reference to revelation in this
correspondence that seems strangely out of step with
everything else we have seen heretofore. Rosenzweig is
speaking about his way of thinking, the germ of
something later developed in his 1925 essay on "The
New Thinking,"[44] and in a letter dated simply
"Saturday" he writes:

    I believe that there are in the life of each
    living thing moments, or perhaps only one
    moment, when it speaks the truth. It may well
    be then, that we need say nothing at all about
    a living thing, but need do no more than
    watch for the moment when this living thing
    expresses itself. The dialogue which these
    monologues form between one another I
    consider to be the whole truth. That they

make a dialogue with one another is the great
secret of the world, the revealing and revealed
secret, yes, the meaning of revelation.[45]

This eloquent passage seems to move in a different
direction from the two approaches we have most
frequently seen; namely, revelation as the breakthrough
of the otherworldly to this world and revelation as
absolute orientation.

THE ROLE OF HISTORY

The new perspective introduced here reveals the
seriousness with which Rosenzweig takes history.
Between the first day of the world and its last day,
there exists the dramatic interlude we call history.
Dialogue is the only form which truth has or can have
during this period; monologues belong to the time
before history's inception or after its completion, to
protology or eschatology.[46] This does not deny the fact
of protological or eschatological truth but it does dictate
its form during this middle period. Nor is there an
implication that this particular mode of truth is better
or worse than truth as it exists before the curtain of
history has been raised or after it has been lowered.
The exigencies of truth are such that this is the only
way it can exist now and "the whole truth is, therefore,
actually contained in history."[47]
    History, then, is the present mode of truth, and
that is why revelation is the way truth exists in the
time of history. The translation by Dorothy Emmet
quoted above speaks of this dialogue being *the meaning
of revelation* but it is significant to note that the
German original is *Inhalt der Offenbarung*, better
translated as "the content of revelation."[48] This is
especially important both because Rosenzweig will later
return to this phrase "the content of revelation" and
because it throws more light on what he is really
saying here. To say that dialogue is the meaning of
revelation might assert nothing more than the fact that

revelation is dialogical. To claim, however, that dialogue is itself the content of revelation is a significantly more radical thesis, since this means positing a noncognitional content of revelation.

In a letter to Martin Buber in 1925, Rosenzweig says that "the primary content of revelation is revelation itself."[49] By translating the same German word (*Inhalt*) with the same English word (*content*), we can better see the thread of continuity between these two utterances separated in time by some nine years. That truth exists the way it does in history is the primary truth which history teaches; that God's truth exists in the mode of history during the time of history is the primary truth contained in revelation. It is not some propositional truth prior or subsequent to history which is the real truth of revelation; rather, this truth consists of the dialogue of history itself. And if the truth of revealed religions is the truth of their revelations, then the validity of these religious communities lies not in their laws or creeds but in their history, their dialogical reality, their life.

Moving beyond the Rosenzweig-Rosenstock correspondence of 1916, we find that his letters in 1917 continue to refer to revelation as orientation in space and time. In writing to Hans Ehrenberg, he makes it clear that the orientation in time is of primary significance:

> The real content of revelation is the de-relativizing of time to absolute history. For the fact that revelation also absolutizes space, forming a firm above and below, a Father in heaven and a people on earth, is only the visible symbol of this.[50]

This explicit recognition of the priority of temporal to spatial orientation is helpful in grasping Rosenzweig's meaning. It is also interesting that he again uses the phrase "content of revelation" in this passage.

But is this language consistent? Is the content of revelation dialogue or orientation? In light of the passages just quoted, the two ideas are synonymous. Dialogue replacing a series of monologues is equivalent to a succession of discrete points being organized through a common referent. It is necessary to explore these two examples, one of speech and one of space, to see their basic unity.

There is a common experience when one enters a room full of people when a discussion is in progress. At first the newcomer hears disconnected pieces of conversation but then, as she becomes aware of the subject under discussion, the isolated monologues begin to come together and can be heard in their connectedness. This happens only because of a larger frame of reference which provides a context of meaning. That the observer can experience this movement from disparate monological utterances to a dialogical continuity is an indication of a broader orientation of meaning. This is what Rosenzweig seems to be alluding to when he says that the existence of dialogue is the great secret of the world *and* the real content of revelation.[51]

Almost everyone who drives has had the experience of looking for a particular address and suddenly becoming disoriented; immediately each corner, each house, each street is a thing in itself, not part of a whole. Then one perceives a referent, a point of orientation, perhaps in some cities it might be the mountains or in others a river or lake. With this perception, everything falls into place; the four points of the compass descend like a grid over the lost driver's location and the whole network of streets and buildings now forms a whole.

The crucial insight here lies in the awareness that the two situations are analogous; meaning and mental map are one. The emergence of monologues into dialogue and of disparate places into a system--these are two signs pointing to the same phenomenon, orientation coming from a larger meaning structure.

The examples considered here refer to a relative orientation in terms of a particular conversational topic or geographical locus. But the fact that all of human history can form a dialogue or that the whole universe can have a symbolic north and south, this can only be in terms of an absolute referent, manifested in but nowise identical with finite experience.

On May 30, 1917 Rosenzweig writes to his friend from childhood, Gertrude Oppenheim:

> For revelation is the foundation of an above and below, a Europe and Asia etc. on the one hand, and on the other hand an early and late, a past and future. The boundless (the Absolute!) steps down to earth and draws revelation from the place of its descent boundaries in the sea of space and the current of time.[52]

The language here presents no new problems. The place of descent is, of course, Sinai; and in light of his earlier comment about the priority of temporal to spatial orientation, we know that Sinai is a symbol of Torah, i.e., the revelation given to Moses on Sinai. Stated one way, Sinai provides a spatial orientation for the whole world. Understood more exactly, the Sinaitic revelation enunciates clearly the overarching theme of history's conversation, the all-encompassing context in terms of which every authentically existing living creature participates in a dialogue containing, in the mode of history, the whole truth.

In the same letter, Rosenzweig differentiates a theology of revelation from pantheism. God is not everything but everything exists from God and towards God, i.e., God stands in relationship to everything.[53] God is "only one thing, the point of the descent, the horizon in which heaven and earth touch."[54] God is not contained in revelation, but revelation is the explicitation of reality's ultimate God-oriented character.

In a later correspondence with Gertrude Oppenheim from August 1917, Rosenzweig returns to this idea and states that God's descent to the world is commandment and promise but not report and description.[55] This avoidance of any identification of revelation and content remains an important aspect of Rosenzweig's theology of revelation.

His correspondence with Rosenstock proves central to his developing thoughts on revelation. In a letter of October 1917, Rosenzweig uses the "I-Thou" language which was later to become a part of the theological mainstream through Buber.[56] In this letter, Rosenzweig speaks of two moments when God says "Thou" to a human being. The first constitutes the being as a creature; it is the "Thou" of God's creative act. Creation, however, happens before one's conscious life; the creature cannot hear the "Thou" which calls it into being. One knows God as Creator only after recognizing God as Revealer.[57]

One month later, Rosenzweig again wrote to Rosenstock. It is not a long letter and in the course of it he says, "I had no desire to write to you because for over a week I was writing something for myself and for Rudi, something very important."[58] This something very important was a letter to Rudolf Ehrenberg, dated November 18, 1917. This chapter began with a reference to that letter and it will now serve as our final guide to this stage of Rosenzweig's thinking about revelation.

THE NUCLEUS OF THE STAR

Here in this nucleus of his *magnum opus*, Rosenzweig talks about "border concepts"[59]--these are the horizons of his thought, serving both as the parameters of his philosophy and the indications of a reality beyond any philosophical system. This is a crucial stage in the development of Rosenzweig's position on revelation. To accomplish what he intends--to show how revelation is different from other kinds of knowing--Rosenzweig must break open the meaning of knowing, especially the forms in which it had hardened in the nineteenth century. And this entails pushing to the limit the ordinary understanding of truth, thereby opening up new perspectives for understanding God, the world, and the human person.

The intellect ordinarily operates in a binary fashion. The awareness of a printed page brings with it the concomitant ability to recognize everything that is *not* a printed page. If being a printed page is *A*, then everything knowable equals either A or not-A. And truth is a matter of formulating accurate equations, properly matching an object and a category--"Yes, what I now have in my hands is a printed page."

Without denying this particular aspect of intellect, Rosenzweig sketches the knowledge situation against a larger horizon, pointing out that there is something self-transcending about the intellect.[60] This translogical (for most systems of logic operate on the binary system described above) dimension of intellect cannot be grasped by the ordinary understanding of truth, precisely because this entails the relation of things which are separate, therefore, somehow two, and, therefore, caught in the same binary system. Rosenzweig seeks a context which precedes separateness and grounds it. There must be a unity prior to all separateness and, therefore, to all conceptualization, precisely because the formation of concepts is based on separation and division. This whole pursuit leads to Rosenzweig's assertion of a truth horizon that is a unity prior to any twoness, a likeness prior to all possible conceptualization with its concomitant binary intellectual activity, in short, a translogical truth.[61] If the truth of revelation belongs to that horizon, then it is indeed different from other forms of knowing.

Truth, then, can be understood in one of two ways. Ordinarily, the term is used to name the identity of two things that are somehow separate: *x* is a printed page. But we also grasp, at least as a limit concept, the realization of a truth preceding the bifurcating function of the intellect whereby the whole world can be categorized as "printed page" or "not printed page." This leads to the understanding of a translogical reality prior to the separating activity of the intellect.[62]

Can something similar be asserted of God? Is there a God before God, a pre-systematic God? Rosenzweig responds in the affirmative, arguing for the limit concept of a "transpersonal godhead." In a letter quoted earlier, Rosenzweig had spoken of the twofold divine address to human beings: creation and revelation. God's revelational word to us means that we can then assimilate the reality of God's prior address in creation. In a deeper sense, revelation gives us the awareness of something prior even to creation, i.e., prior to the inception of time, differentiation (creation is described in the Bible as initially a work of separation),   and   conceptualization   (the   binary awareness of good *and* evil signalling the first parents' transition to the human condition outside of the garden now forever to be barred to them). Revelation, though always appropriated within history, is itself the horizon of history and of humankind;   it is our awareness of the real horizon of our existence, a pre-systematic life with God. This is the awareness which Rosenzweig believes the Psalmist had in mind when he wrote: "I am always with You". (*Psalm* 73:23)

What the psalm asserts is the human horizon, our transhistorical being-with-God.   Understood as the response in faith to the divine revelation of the horizon of human existence, specifically, one's own existence, these words are the key to Rosenzweig's theology of revelation.

In this context, it is possible to discern the meaning of a difficult but important passage in the *Urzelle*:

What I'm claiming now is that all that happens between the Absolute and the Relative "before" is revelation and all that happens "after" is Nature, world or whatever you want to call it. This is just a first approach to this idea, of course, nothing further. That it is not more is clear from the fact that the two relations cannot be so antithetically opposed as is suggested here, for although the Absolute does indeed stand in relationship to the Relative after, it is essential for the Relative before, that the Absolute at first stands in no relationship to the Relative as such, but that the Relative stands as it is, dust and ashes, but nevertheless on its own feet.[63]

The meaning of this passage is not transparent but we have at hand the elements for understanding it.

Of first significance is the realization that, although the experience of revelation comes to the human recipients at some specific point in their conscious life, the realm of revelation is the horizonal existence of human beings, their life with God before time. This helps to elucidate the otherwise confusing statement of Rosenzweig that revelation is somehow before the world. Secondly, there is another suggestion of two stages of development. This entails a time when the human person seems to be standing without relationship and on her own feet. And this is followed by a time of explicitated relationship between God and the human person. The backdrop for this is the recovery of the "I" that Rosenzweig sees as an essential part of his thought.

Rosenzweig speaks of the *Urzelle* as his Archimedes point, the proverbial position from which one can move the world.[64] But what world does Rosenzweig feel constrained to move? The world of the Hegelian system where revelation had been co-opted, i.e., the name had been retained but the reality was emptied of meaning. Idealism has no room for the relationship of "I" and "Thou" because of its penchant for subsuming all differences into a systematic identity.

Philosophy--and for Rosenzweig this means the
Greek enterprise culminating in Hegel--is a system
which gradually swallows up the individual. Unless the
individual takes stock and realizes that, however
unimportant he might be from the perspective of the
system, however much any theory may reduce him to a
mere instantiation of some universal, it is he, this same
individual, who had the shamelessness to philosophize,
to think the system.[65] So she may be but dust and
ashes but she is nonetheless there; it is this same
individual, with first and family name, who not only
philosophizes but...izes, exists.[66]

This existing individual, satisfied with his own
self-identity, does not automatically seek a relationship
with God; it is God who seeks a relationship with just
such a free human person. Or rather, God prompts
such a person to remember the relationship that makes
it possible for him to be an "I"--the horizon of his
experience, the limit concept of his presystematic life--in
a word, revelation.[67] Revelation is not the third person
knowledge that one belongs to a certain genus, or even
that one is a creature of God. Understood in the third
person, even God is a part of the System. But
systematic knowledge--with all its definitions and
categories--does not give the world any ultimate
orientation, unless third-person truth is itself grounded
in translogical reality, related to a transpersonal God in
the transhistorical mystery of revelation. This is
precisely what Rosenzweig has been saying from the
beginning: real orientation comes from revelation.

Real orientation and, therefore, participation in real
life only begins with the experience of being an "I"
responding to the God who calls one as a "Thou."[68] The
individual still sleeping in egotism or lost in the woods
of the System is ineluctably caught in relativism, but
the individual attuned to the relationship preceding it
from all eternity--its horizonal existence with God--has
been awakened by revelation and enabled to assimilate
being a creature. It is this enlivened and enlightened

person who can now be commanded to love and thereby participate in the redemptive work still to be done. This dialogically alive "I" can be the center of the world, the little plot of ground between four tent poles which has the capacity to grow as large as the world itself.[69] This "I" knows a truth not contained by the System or any third-person proposition; thus its knowledge is distinguished from all other forms of human knowing. This is the real answer to Rosenzweig's preoccupying question about the difference between revelation and all philosophical knowledge. As Gertrude Horwitz has observed:

The content of revelation is neither rational knowledge nor factual information; rather, it is the speech between God and man, speech based on mutual love.[70]

Or, as Guy Petitdemange has indicated, revelation in Rosenzweig does not give us new knowledge but leads us rather into the school of time and speech.[71] Here indeed is the nucleus of Rosenzweig's theology of revelation in *The Star of Redemption*.

Rosenzweig's basic understanding of revelation does not change after this initial direction is established. If revelation is ultimately a knowledge question, then it seems impossible to get beyond the dilemma of competing and contradictory knowledge statements, e.g., the Messiah has come; the Messiah has not come. If, on the other hand, revelation establishes not new knowledge but new relationship, then the possibility emerges of two different, but not necessarily competitive, modes of relationship. This, in turn, opens up the possibility of new forms of Jewish-Christian dialogue.

CHAPTER TWO

NOTES

1. Franz Rosenzweig, *Zweistromland* (The Hague: Martinas Nijhoff Publisher, 1984), p. 125.

2. A general introduction can be found in Isaac Husik, *A History of Medieval Jewish Philosophy* (New York: Atheneum, 1969), pp. 23-47. Since Sura was the chief center of Jewish learning at that time, Saadia was the intellectual leader of the Jewish community of his day. Alexander Altmann has an excellent treatment of Saadia's theory of revelation in his *Studies in Religious Philosophy and Mysticism* (Ithica, NY: Cornell University Press, 1969), pp. 140-160.

3. Saadia Gaon, *Beliefs and Opinions*, trans. from the Arabic and Hebrew by Samuel Rosenblatt (New Haven: Yale University Press, 1948), p. 16.

4. Saadia Gaon, *Beliefs and Opinions*, p. 18.

5. Saadia Gaon, *Beliefs and Opinions*, p. 32.

6. Saadia Gaon, *Beliefs and Opinions*, p. 138. On p. 148 he goes on to quote Exodus 4:30 & 31, seeing this as a general pattern for belief: "And Aaron spoke all the words which the Lord had given Moses, and *did the signs* in the sight of the people. *And the people believed. . . .*" (italics my own).

7. This is taken from Maimonides' introduction to *Mishne Torah* in *A Maimonides Reader*, ed. by Isadore Twersky (New York: Behrman house, 1972), p. 35.

8. *A Maimonides Reader.* p. 36.

9. Philo, *On the Decalogue*, trans. by F. H. Colson, vol. 7 of the Loeb edition (Cambridge: Harvard University Press, 1968), p.23.

10. Judah Halevi, *The Kuzari*, trans. from the Arabic by Hartwig Hirschfeld with the introduction by Henry Slonimsky (New York: Schocken, 1964), p. 63.

11. S. L. Steinheim, *Die Offenbarung nach dem Lehrbegriff der Synagoge* (Frankfurt a. M.: n.p., 1835), Part One, p. 88.

12. see chap. one, footnote 9.

13. Rosenzweig, *Briefe und Tagebücher*, I-1, p. 87.

14. Rosenzweig, *Briefe und Tagebücher*, I-1, p. 48. Translation my own.

15. The most available English source for filling in some of the details of this period can be found in Glatzer, *Franz Rosenzweig: His Life and Thought*, pp, 1-22.

16. Glatzer. *Franz Rosenzweig: His Life and Thought*, p. 31.

17. Rosenzweig, *Zweistromland*, pp. 687-697.

18. Robert G. Goldy and H. Frederick Holch published an English translation of this work in 1968 in the Canadian Journal of Theology, volume XVI, No. 2.

19. Rosenzweig, *Zweistromland*, p. 125.

20. *Judaism Despite Christianity*, ed. Dorothy Emmet, trans. by Eugen Rosenstock-Huessy (New York: Schoken Books, 1969), p. 94.

21. Rosenstock-Huessy, *Judaism Despite Christianity*, p. 104.

22. Rosenzweig, *Zweistromland*, p. 128. Translation my own.

23. Rosenzweig, *Zweistromland*, p. 691.

24. Rosenzweig, *Zweistromland*, p. 692.

25. Rosenzweig, *Zweistromland*, p. 693.

26. Rosenzweig, *Zweistromland*, p. 691.

27. Rosenzweig, *Zweistromland*, p. 693. Translation my own.

28. Rosenzweig, *Zweistromland*, p. 693.

29. The letter on October 31, 1913 to Rudolf Ehrenberg is the source of this information. It can be found in Rosenzweig, *Briefe und Tagebücher*, I-1, pp. 132-138. A large portion of this letter can also be found in Glatzer, *Franz Rosenzweig: His Life and Thought*, p. 28 and pp. 341-344.

30. Rosenzweig, *Zweistromland*, p. 127. Translation my own.

31. Rosenzweig, *Briefe und Tagebücher*, I-1, p. 322. Translation my own.

32. Rosenstock-Huessy, *Judaism Despite Christianity*, p. 74.

33. Rosenstock-Huessy, *Ja und Nein: Autobiographische Fragmente* (Heidelberg: Verlag Lambert Schneider, 1968), p. 170. Translation my own.

34. Rosenstock-Huessy, *Judaism Despite Christianity*, p. 114.

35. Rosenstock-Huessy, *Judaism Despite Christianity*, p. 117.

36. Rosenstock-Huessy, *Judaism Despite Christianity*, p. 19.

37. Rosenstock-Huessy, *Judaism Despite Christianity*, p. 120.

38. Rosenstock-Huessy, *Judaism Despite Christianity*, p. 122.

39. Rosenstock-Huessy, *Judaism Despite Christianity*, p. 124.

40. Rosenstock-Huessy, *Judaism Despite Christianity*, p. 132.

41. Rosenstock-Huessy, *Judaism Despite Christianity*, p. 160.

42. Rosenstock-Huessy, *Judaism Despite Christianity*, p. 165.

43. Rosenstock-Huessy, *Judaism Despite Christianity*, p. 166.

44. Rosenzweig, *Zweistromland*, pp. 139-161.

45. Rosenstock-Huessy, *Judaism Despite Christianity*, pp. 147-8.

46. Rosenstock-Huessy, *Judaism Despite Christianity*, p. 148.

47. Rosenstock-Huessy, *Judaism Despite Christianity*, p. 149.

48. Rosenzweig, *Briefe und Tagebücher*, I-1, p. 292.

49. Rosenzweig, *On Jewish Learning*, p. 118. The original German is on p. 1040 of Rosenzweig, *Briefe und Tagebücher*, I-2.

50. Rosenzweig, *Briefe und Tagebücher*, I-1, p. 358. Translation my own.

51. Rosenzweig, *Briefe und Tagebücher*, I-1, p. 292.

52. Rosenzweig, *Briefe und Tagebücher*, I-1, p. 413. Translation my own.

53. Rosenzweig, *Briefe und Tagebücher*, I-1, p.414.

54. Rosenzweig, *Briefe und Tagebücher*, I-1, p.414. Translation my own.

55. Rosenzweig, *Briefe und Tagebücher*, I-1, p. 426.

56. The I-Thou language often is known only through Martin Buber's published book of that name in 1923. But it is well to be reminded of the comment of Bernhard Casper: "Allein, wenn wir uns nur ein wenig genauer in der Geschichte umschauen, so zeigt sich alsbald, dass 'Ich und Du' keineswegs ein Anfang war, ein Keim, in dem wir das dialogische Denken sozusagen in seiner Reinheit greifen könnten. Bubers bekanntes Werk ist viel eher ein Ende, eine bereits reife Frucht." This quotation is from p. 17 of the excellent study by Bernhard Casper, *Das Dialogische Denken* (Freiburg: Herder, 1967).

57. Rosenzweig, *Briefe und Tagebücher*, I-1, p. 471.

58. Rosenzweig, *Briefe und Tagebücher*, I-1, p. 481. Translation my own.

59. Rosenzweig, *Zweistromland*, p. 135.

60. Rosenzweig, *Zweistromland*, p. 136.

61. Rosenzweig, *Zweistromland*, p. 136.

62. Rosenzweig, *Zweistromland*, p. 137.

63. Rosenzweig, *Zweistromland*, p. 129. Translation my own.

64. Rosenzweig, *Zweistromland*, p. 125.

65. Rosenzweig, *Zweistromland*, p. 127.

66. Rosenzweig, *Zweistromland*, P. 127.

67. Rosenzweig, *Zweistromland*, p. 131.

68. Rosenzweig, *Zweistromland*, p. 136.

69. Rosenzweig, *Zweistromland*, p. 137.

70. This is from p. 16 of her microfilmed dissertation, "Speech and time in the Philosophy of Franz Rosenzweig", Bryn Mawr College, 1963.

71. I am using the German version of the address which appeared in two installments (March and June 1974) in *Judaica* with the title "Existenz und Offenbarung in den ersten Werken von Franz Rosenzweig."

CHAPTER THREE

THE STAR OF REDEMPTION

It would be difficult to exaggerate the importance of the *The Star of Redemption* in Rosenzweig's self-understanding. As a soldier on the Balkan front in September 1918 Rosenzweig writes to his cousin Rudolf Ehrenberg that he has begun a book which will be his system, that this book evolved from a letter he had written to this same cousin in November 1917 (the *Urzelle*), and that he finds himself now, after fourteen days into the writing of his book, still deluged by the ideas pouring into his head.[1] In a preeminent sense, this was to be *his book*, the unique and unrepeatable expression of his being.

Rosenzweig notes exactly the period during which the book was written, from August 22, 1918 to February 16, 1919.[2] In less than six months, under the far from ideal circumstances of writing on military postcards from the eastern front of the First World War, he produces a work which gives expression to the core insights of his experience. Nor does he fail to recognize the significance of what he has done, for he writes enthusiastically to Martin Buber that he has the unavoidable feeling of having brought together in this one book the fullness of his spiritual existence, that everything he would later write would be a matter of appendices, and that his real future would now be much more in living than in writing.[3]

This sense of deep satisfaction and accomplishment was not just a thing of the moment. Two years after

55

the completion of the book he writes to Gertrude
Oppenheim:

> I can really be thankful for my fate. How
> many people have the opportunity, at the age
> of thirty-two, to see the realization of the
> wildest dream of their youth? It's what my
> fifteen years of doubt were all about, to know
> that I have finished and behind me a work
> that is really eternal (at least, eternal in the
> human way we use that word). My further life
> is now really a great bonus; that's something
> that Goethe could say only on his
> eighty-second birthday when he had put the
> final touches on his *Faust*."[4]

Within a few months of writing this letter, Rosenzweig
noticed the first symptoms of the disease which was to
lead him to an early and painful death.[5] Much more
than he realized when he wrote this letter, his further
life was indeed to be a bonus.

In an important essay of 1925 entitled "The New
Thinking" Rosenzweig reflects on the *The Star of
Redemption* and the reactions it has prompted from the
time of its publication.[6] His *magnum opus*, as
Rosenzweig speaks about it now in retrospect, is not a
book of Jewish theology nor a book on the philosophy of
religion but a system of philosophy.[7] To know that
Rosenzweig understands himself to be doing philosophy,
to be aware of this movement from the old to the new
way of thinking, to realize that revelation is not
tangential to this philosophical revolution but
constitutive of it, these are some of our immediate
objectives.

For Rosenzweig, the old way of philosophizing is
that which stretches form Ionia to Jena, from the
pre-Socratics to Hegel. Its three main phases are
characterized by the object studied: the world (ancient
philosophy), God (medieval philosophy) and the human
person (modern philosophy). In all of these stages,

philosophy's goal remained the same, to find the essence of what is, and to be able to conclude with a resounding proclamation that everything is essentially something else, whether this be water or air, matter or spirit, divine or human consciousness.[8]

From Rosenzweig's perspective, this whole enterprise has grounded to a halt and necessarily so. He is not persuaded by the presupposition that the essence of what is can be rationally understood. Nor does he believe that diverse realities are ultimately one. The rapid juggling of these three elements of world, human person, and God until they seem to be one creates nothing more than an illusion. Experience exposes the monistic system as sleight of hand, showing that each of the elements is separate and irreducible. "But experience, no matter how deeply it probes, will find only the human in man, the worldly in the world, and the godly in God."[9] With this discovery, philosophy has not reached its end but has found a new beginning, not as cognitive philosophy but as experiencing philosophy.[10]

The old philosophy of analytical thinking about essences and competing reductionism is dead and the new philosophy of experience and encounter, of speech and time, has been born. Rosenzweig does not claim to be its parent;his own thinking has been enabled by the work of others--Schelling and Feuerbach, Cohen and Rosenstock.[11] In regard to the central section of *The Star of Redemption*, our own focus in this chapter, Rosenzweig acknowledges his co-workers in the vineyard of dialogical thought: Martin Buber and Ferdinand Ebner.[12]

The mention of *The Star*'s central section requires a brief consideration of its architectonic. The book has three sections, each of which has an introduction and three chapters. In the first section are to be found the elements of his system: God, world, and the human person. Their relationships are studied in the second section: creation, revelation and redemption. The third section deals with their final shape: fire, rays, and star.

Rosenzweig states that it is for this reason that the title is itself an attempt to bring together the content of the three sections: the elements, their course, and the resulting form.[13]

The seriousness with which time is taken and the extent to which it is constitutive of a philosophy indicates its proximity to Rosenzweig's concept of "new thinking." Thus the sectional divisions of *The Star* parallel temporal perspectives. The story of the past is found in the first section, as the future is in the third. But the story of the present is in the second section and it cannot really be a story because of that genre's implication of a third person narrative. Just as the proper tense of the second section is the present, its proper grammatical person is the second person singular, the language of "thou."[14]

Nowhere is time taken more seriously than in genuine dialogue, i.e., dialogue where the participants do not know ahead of time what their partners will say or, more importantly, even what they themselves will say. Rosenzweig's new thinking calls for a speech-thinker (*Sprachdenker*), a philosopher capable of dialogue, a thinker for whom a partner in thought is necessary. The old thinking, from the pre-Socratics to Hegel, was an isolated and isolating activity, a thinking for no one and a speaking to no one.[15] It was a thought experiment conducted inside the laboratory of logic. Under the interactional conditions of real life, the experiment proved incapable of reduplication. Real life would not hold still for it; this was its ineluctable deficiency.

The second chapter of the second section of *The Star* deserves to be understood philosophically as well as structurally as the heart of Rosenzweig's entire work, because it is there in the relational reality of revelation that philosophy manifests itself most clearly as speech-thinking. It is there Rosenzweig sought most deliberately to employ "eine Methode des Erzählens," a method of story-telling, of narrative thinking, of dialogue.[16] Stories have nouns but they are not of central importance; attention is focused on the verbs, the words expressing time. Time is part of truth--this is the element never adequately understood in the logic laboratories of earlier European thought. The three chapters of the first section of *The Star* could have been arranged in any order. There was no intrinsic necessity for discussing God before world or world before humanity. For the first section dealt with the unrelated elements, the mere essences, and "essences do not want to know anything about time."[17] In the second section, the progression of the story from creation to revelation and redemption constitutes the truth to be communicated--how the elements relate, what they do and what happens to them, who speaks and who responds--this is precisely the new thinking itself.

ADAM'S DIALOGUE WITH GOD

The focal point of our study is the dialogue of revelation; especially in this attempt to understand revelation, the maintenance of the dialogical perspective is crucial. It is in the Bible that Rosenzweig sees the unfolding of revelational reality. It is not that the Bible is too unsophisticated to rise to the level of abstractions and logical argumentation, but rather that the very depth of its religious genius is contained in its use of the dialogical form. Three of the biblical dialogues provide the program of our subsequent investigations in this chapter: Adam's dialogue with God in the garden, Moses' dialogue with the divine presence in the burning bush, and the lovers' dialogue in the Song of Songs.
It is in the early chapters of Genesis that Rosenzweig finds a model for the revelational discourse which is pre-historical, both for the human race and for every individual human being. In the first eleven chapters of Genesis, Israel reaches back to the time before its conscious remembrances, for its real history begins with chapter twelve. Like adults trying to reconstruct their first two years of life, snatching

images from that distant time and fleshing them out
with later powers of speech and thought, so does Israel
tell the pre-history of the human family from the
perspective of her mature experience of a living God.
The dialogue with Adam is a paradigm for the seed of
revelational reality buried in the soil of the human
consciousness, waiting for that later dialogical
encounter which will cause it to be recollected and
recognized as a primordial revelation.

Rosenzweig's starting point is a protological myth
prior even to the one found in the Genesis saga of
Adam and Eve.[18] The protology of the Bible describes
archetypal parents in a garden-world, not yet aware of
the dichotomies of adult life: good and evil, rest and
work, maleness and femaleness. Rosenzweig's myth is
even more ultimate because it pushes back to the inner
life of God before he called his creatures to authentic
dialogue; in this protological time, no authentic
"I-Thou" relationship exists. This is the hypothetical
time before time, a stasis of unrelated elements: the
concealed God, the material world, the self-contained
human being.

In Genesis 3:9, God asks Adam, "Where are you?"
Interestingly enough, the quest for the Thou does not
immediately eventuate in the discovery of what is
sought, but in the finding of the seeker. "The I
discovers itself at the moment when it asserts the
existence of the Thou by inquiring into its Where."[19] So
the story is not about the discovery of Adam's self but
of God's.

Adam is not ready for this encounter. He flees to
the safer world of the third person: "The woman you
put at my side--she gave me of the tree, and I ate."
(Genesis 3:12) This "Thou" is not the authentic Thou of
dialogue, only its semantic imitation; man remains
hidden and blames the woman. The woman transfers
the blame to what Rosenzweig identifies as the
ultimate It.[20] She says, "The serpent duped me, and I
ate." (Genesis 3:13)

God's address to Adam underpins Rosenzweig's theology of revelation; he states explicitly that the continual renewal of this primeval revelation is the content of the second section of *The Star of Redemption*.[21] In a letter to Eva Ehrenberg in 1924, he writes that the revelation of the Creator to Adam is the soul of religion and therefore the soul of all the religions which are its body.[22] All human beings have the potential of revelatory experience; every person has the possibility of becoming a Thou. But this has never been consciously articulated or given historical form except in the biblical faiths of Judaism and Christianity; the new thinking is Jewish or Christian only to the extent that these two historical religions are capable of renewing this revelation to Adam.

For Rosenzweig, the truth of what is going on between God and humanity finds expression only in the historical religions of biblical faith, Judaism and Christianity, but this does not prevent authentic revelatory experience from happening elsewhere. However objectively invalid a particular religious rite may be, every person in prayer retains the freedom to answer with honesty and authenticity the question prototypically addressed to Adam.

Did God wait for Mt. Sinai or, perhaps, Golgotha? No paths that lead from Sinai to Golgotha are guaranteed to lead to him, but neither can he possibly have failed to come to one who sought him on the trails skirting Olympus. There is no temple built so close to him as to give man reassurance in its closeness, and none is so far from him as to make it too difficult for man's hand to reach. There is no direction from which it would not be possible for him to come, and none from which he must come; no block of wood in which he may not once take up his dwelling, and no psalm of David that will always reach his ear.[23]

The historical form articulates what really goes on but reality can happen without articulation and articulation can be hollow without the reality it attempts to express.

Religion and the new thinking or true philosophy coincide when they connect with the way reality is happening. Rosenzweig maintains that the Bible is different from all other books because you can know the Bible either by reading it (which is the only way of knowing other books) or by listening to the human heart. "The Bible and the heart say the same thing; it is because of this, and only because of this, that the Bible is revelation."[24] He makes a similar point in a letter to his mother, telling her that what is crucial is not "believing in the good Lord" but opening up one's five senses and looking at reality, entertaining the dangerous possibility that one might indeed be met there by God.[25]

In summary, then, historical religions can lay claim to valid revelational traditions only because of the prior mystery of religion by which they are first grasped. Religion exists because of a primordial connectedness between God and the human heart, a horizon in which God and the human person are already together in such a way that they have space to be near or far from each other. Within this horizon people have experiences which lead them to call themselves religious or atheist, pantheist or agnostic, but all of this takes place against a backdrop of God's question to Adam, God's quest for his own dialogical existence and for a partner in dialogue.

MOSES' DIALOGUE WITH GOD

Lest it seem in any way that Rosenzweig is merely encouraging subjective religious experience, the divine encounter with Adam must be seen in conjunction with God's dialogue with Moses. This latter encounter has two foci: the revelation of the divine name and the giving of the Torah, a path of law and commandment. One might wonder why Rosenzweig concerns himself with the past of biblical history. God's dialogue with Adam seems to indicate that human beings, simply by reason of their humanness, stand on the threshold of revelational reality. Consequently, one might ask why the encumbrances of historical religions are required at all. If the Bible is no more than what the human heart already knows and belief in God no more than opening up one's five senses to the divine presence, then why is there any need for Judaism or Christianity or any other historical manifestation of a divine mystery? Rosenzweig's theology offers a double answer to this question. First, he would answer in terms of the grounding of present experience in the past and, second, he would stress the importance of commandment in the revelational reality.

"The Presentness of the miracle of revelation is and remains its content; its historicity, however, is its ground and its warrant."[26] This succinct statement from *The Star* reveals the middle ground which Rosenzweig's position occupies; he will not reduce the content of revelation to the static elements of history surviving within religion as laws or dogmas. He insists that revelation's content is presentness, but, on the other hand, he refuses to identify revelation with every kind of subjective experience laying claim to contact with the divine mystery. What emerges is something of a check-and-balance or bicameral dynamic in Rosenzweig's thought. The experience of revelation must show its warranty in terms of history. Historical forms, on the other hand, must constantly be challenged to translate themselves into present experience, just as present experience is continually required to demonstrate its continuity with the historical forms.

The last chapter included extensive discussion of the role of orientation in Rosenzweig's understanding of revelation. He does not abandon this current of insight in *The Star*:

"In the intricate world of things there was no
midpoint or beginning at all; the I, however,
together with its proper name, introduces these
concepts of midpoint and beginning into the
world. . . . The I longs for orientation, for a
world which does not just lie there in any old
arrangement, nor flow past in any old
sequence, but a world which supports the
inner order inherent in the I's experience on
the solid base of an external order."[27]

The individual experience could drown on the shoals of
subjectivism unless its own orientation can be given
through a light on the shore, something which itself is
not at sea. And for Rosenzweig, this ground of revelation, providing both midpoint in space and in time, is
the revelation of the divine name.[28]

In 1917, the same year in which Rosenzweig
conceived the core insight which grew into *The Star of
Redemption*, he wrote to Gertrude Oppenheim that a
static divine presence, a mere eternal being of God,
would not be of great benefit to human beings. The
classic translation of Exodus 3:14 as "I am who I am"
seems to Rosenzweig to be a Greek betrayal of the
original Hebrew meaning, "I am with you as I was with
your forefathers."[29]

In the year of his death, Rosenzweig returned to
this theme of the divine name in an essay entitled "The
Eternal One."[30]   The title is a reference to Moses
Mendelssohn's translation of the text of Exodus 3:14--"I
am the Being, who is eternal."[31]   In understanding this
text as referring to God's timeless essence, Rosenzweig
judges Mendelssohn to have been too strongly
influenced by the rationalist and neoclassical spirit of
his century.   He argues that the text should be
translated: "I will be there as the one who will be there
and you shall tell the children of Israel: 'I am There
sends me to you.'"[32]   This is the kernel of biblical
revelation; this cry of "I will be there" from the burning

bush identifies once and for all the God of creation with the God who is encountered in the presentness of revelation; this is the grounding in space and time which individual revelational experience demands.

Moses is worthy to hear the divine name because he fulfills the task which Adam was unprepared to meet; Adam hid from the divine address, not only behind fig leaves, but behind rationalizations and third-person accusations. Our first parent proved irresponsible, i.e., he was not able to respond. But when Moses heard God calling his name from the burning bush, he answers "Here I am" (Exodus 3:4). This response (in Hebrew, *hineni*) implies the full taking of responsibility, for it is not only an indication of presence, of being there, but a sign of willingness for service.

God identifies himself in this encounter as "the God of your fathers, the God of Abraham, the God of Isaac, and the God of Jacob" (Exodus 3:6). Moses is shown to be a true son of Abraham, his father. The twenty-second chapter of Genesis, the powerful account of the *Akedah*, the binding of Isaac, contains not only the opening *hineni* of Abraham to God's call (v. 1) but Abraham's painful *hineni* to the son whom he believes he must sacrifice (v. 7) and his hopeful *hineni* to the angel of the Lord who stays his hand and relieves this father of his tragic task (v. 11).

The receptivity and the readiness of Moses reveal Abraham as his ancestor in more than blood. Abraham is indeed the father of a people, the first Jew, the patriarch *par excellence*, called to be responsible to the divine address, called to be there and to be ready for service. The dialogue between Moses and the God of Abraham discloses the contraction of revelation from humankind as a whole, the address to Adam, to a particular religion and people, to a point in time and space, to history.

The orientation through history which is symbolized in the divine name requires our concern with the past. The other reason has to do with commandment.

Rosenzweig addresses this topic in the second section of *The Star*, and it is our other focus in considering the dialogical encounter between God and Moses. For Rosenzweig, religious experience is not an end in itself. Authentic revelatory experience does not terminate in mere ecstasy or enlightenment any more than it does in propositional knowledge or dogma. What is revealed in revelation is the divine name, i.e., the awareness that the God who is far is the God who is near, that the God of creation knows you by name, that the divine mystery is presence and presentness. The awareness of God being with us is at the same time the voice of commandment, just as the human *hineni* contains a readiness to obey as well as an acknowledgement of being there.

According to Rosenzweig, the commandment received in revelation is single. And it is the commandment to love. "God's first word to the soul that unlocks itself to him is 'love me!'"[33] This, of course, is Israel's central profession of faith, given classic expression in the fifth book of Moses (Deuteronomy 6:4-5): "Hear, O Israel, the Lord is our God, The Lord alone. You shall love the Lord your God with all your heart and with all your soul and with all your might." This commandment is not merely the highest but essentially the *only* commandment, the sum and substance of all commandments spoken by God.[34] The idea of a commandment to love contains a problem, however, and Rosenzweig does not fail to notice it. How can love be commanded? Must it not of its very nature be a free response? Rosenzweig writes: "Yes of course, love cannot be commanded. No third party can command it or extort it. No third party can, but the One can. The commandment of love can only proceed from the mouth of the lover. Only the lover can and does say: 'love me!--and he really does so."[35] It is precisely because revelation is a dialogue and not a dogma that it has the right to speak in the second person, in the imperative.

The distinction Rosenzweig makes between commandment (*Gebot*) and law (*Gesetz*) is crucial at this point. "Law reckons with times, with a future, with duration. The commandment knows only the moment; it awaits the result in the very instant of its promulgation. . . . Thus the commandment is purely the present."[36] Understanding the function of presentness in Rosenzweig's revelational theology, it follows that only the commandment and not law can properly belong to revelation.

Again it is the middle way which Rosenzweig seeks. He walks a path which excludes both a subjectivity uprooted from history and a tradition removed from presentness. He rejects both religious anarchy, a free-floating cult of personal religious experience, and a sterile submission to observance, a soulless legalism. He writes to Martin Buber:

"God is not a Law-giver. But He commands. It is only by the manner of his observance that man in his inertia changes the commandments into Law, a legal system with paragraphs..."[37]

By presentness, attentiveness, openness to the divine address, we can turn law back into commandment.

The interpretative third-person statement of law ("it is forbidden to . . .") can be transformed into the dialogical reality of commandment ("thou shalt. . .") --this is part of the dynamic quality of Rosenzweig's understanding of revelation. As he states in another letter to Buber: "Even for him who observes the Law, revelation is not what you call law-giving. 'On this day'--that is his theory of experience as well as yours. . . . We do not consciously accept the fact that every commandment can become law, but that the law can always be changed back into a commandment."[38] This is the challenge to the observant Jew. It is the way of Torah.

In a letter written in 1924 to Isaac Breuer, Rosenzweig admits that his treatment of the Law in

The Star of Redemption was too brief.[39]   Rosenzweig
cites two reasons for this--first, that in presenting
Judaism and Christianity through a parallel treatment,
he could not have commented on Jewish law more
extensively without having correspondingly said more
about Christian dogma; but, secondly, that he was not
ready then (1918-1919) nor now (1924) to really discuss
the Law at any length. And then Rosenzweig gives us a
glimpse of the course along which he thought his life
might have moved, had he not received the diagnosis of
a terminal disease. "When I finished *The Star*, I
thought that I was beginning decades of learning and
living, teaching and studying, and that perhaps at the
very end, when I would be quite old, then one more
book would appear, and that would have been a book
about the Law."[40]   We see here both Rosenzweig's love
for the Law and the unfinished character of his
involvement with it.

Rosenzweig openly acknowledges the human
element in the formulation of religious law. "Revelation
is certainly not Law-giving; it is only this: revelation.
The primary content of revelation is revelation itself.
'He came down' (on Sinai)--this already concludes the
revelation; 'He spoke' is the beginning of interpretation,
and certainly 'I am.' But where does this 'interpretation'
stop being legitimate?"[41]   What Rosenzweig finally
admits in this same letter is that he, too, is hesitant to
see revelation pinned down anywhere by human
interpretation.   Because he views Judaism and
Christianity as true religions, he is ready to concede
that both of them are exceptions--Christianity in its
identification of revelation with a human person and
Judaism with its claim to a law unlike other laws.[42]

The struggle between law and commandment is not
ended at the time of Rosenzweig's death. His life is a
wrestling with this dialectic. On the one hand, an
increasing preoccupation with the Law; on the other
hand, firm insistence that "Judaism *is* *not* law; it
creates law but it *is* *not* identical with it; Judaism is
being a Jew."[43]   Rosenzweig refuses to solve his

dilemma by surrendering to one side of it. In this same letter of 1922 to Rudolf Hallo, he states explicitly that he will not be caught on the fork of an all-or-nothing option. "What belongs to us is neither everything nor nothing; what belongs to us is something."[44] That something is the great dialogue between God and Moses, Torah in its most all-inclusive sense, interpreted and developed as a legal code and eternally capable of being transformed back again into presentness, dialogue, and the commandment to love.

It is within the dynamics of this same commandment to love that Rosenzweig locates his theology of sin and repentance. The catalogs of sins found in traditional Judaism and Christianity alike are of no use to him. These fail the criterion of presentness. They are third-person categorizations, too far from the reality of dialogue. What, then, is the existential reality of sin? The person called to love realizes that even in the presentness of the revelatory moment he does not love nearly as much as he is loved.[45] This leads to a shame that can be abolished only by the admission "I have sinned," and by the even deeper realization, "I am a sinner."[46] For Rosenzweig, there is no further need of absolution; when a person admits and accepts God's love and at the same time takes on the responsibility for whatever his own love lacks, then the dialogue of repentance and forgiveness is complete.

For many, a primary product of religion is guilt. Much of what comes from the traditions of Judaism and Christianity seems to foster guilt, yet guilt has no place and no religious significance at all in a theology like Rosenzweig's. Guilt is a psychological phenomenon-- a product of our socialization for monitoring behavior. Sorrow, on the other hand, stems from a sense of personal involvement and taking responsibility for our relationships and our free actions in a faithful context. Guilt can function prior to any real faith experience or properly religious existence; sorrow, on the other hand, comes only after a degree of spiritual maturation, implying the whole revelatory dialogue of love which Rosenzweig describes. And it is sorrow which leads to repentance and forgiveness.

THE SONG OF SONGS

Having examined the protological address to Adam and the fuller rhythm of call, trust, commandment, sorrow, sin, and repentance in God's dialogue with Moses, it remains for us to consider the lovers' dialogue found in Song of Songs. For many scripture scholars it is a matter of some embarrassment that this book of love poetry was ever included in the biblical canon. So it is not without some surprise that one reads in Rosenzweig: "We have recognized the Song of Songs as the focal book of revelation."[47]

In the opening chapters of this book we find a progression which parallels Rosenzweig's reflections on revelation. This can be traced in the opening cry of the beloved for her lover and the response of the lover to her pleading:

Oh, give me of the kisses of your mouth, for your love is more delightful than wine. Your ointments yield a sweet fragrance; your name is like finest oil.

(The Song of Songs 1:2 & 3)

Our attention here is directed to the kiss, the mouth, and the word.

Speaking of the configuration of the Star as a human countenance, Rosenzweig sees the first triangle as formed by the forehead (to which belongs the nose) and the cheeks (to which belong the ears). This is the triangle of the receptive organs. A second triangle, superimposed on this first one, is formed by the two eyes and the mouth. These are the active organs of the face. The eyes shine with the communicative power which is then given a two-fold expression through the mouth: the word and the kiss.[48]

Returning now to the lines of the text, we note that the beloved knows the name of her lover and she is asking now for the kiss of his mouth. He who has already heard her voice (the passive triangle of his countenance) is asked now to see her and kiss her (the active triangle of his countenance). And yet, he is already her lover and, therefore, we can presume that he has been active towards her before. To understand this is to be in touch with the basic revelational reality: how it is a matter of relationship and not static essence, dialogue not dogma, presence not cognitive content or calculation, both a word and a kiss, both a plea and an acceptance, a rediscovery in the present of the initiative-taking love which was already there in the past.

The words of the lover in the second chapter constitute a song of love and springtime. Springtime, of course, is the season of revelation, because the prophecy contained in the winter existence of nature is fulfilled in the second creation or revelation of spring:

My beloved spoke thus to me,
'Arise, my darling:
My fair one, come away!
For now the winter is past,
The rains are over and gone.
The blossoms have appeared in the land,
The time of pruning has come;
The song of the turtledove Is heard in our land.
The green figs form on the fig tree,
The vines in blossom give off fragrance.
Arise, my darling; My fair one, come away!
O my dove, in the cranny of the rocks,
Hidden by the cliff,
Let me see your face,
Let me hear your voice;
For your voice is sweet
And your face is comely?'
                    (The Song of Songs, 2:10-14)

Several themes which are germane to Rosenzweig's understanding of revelation can be discerned in this text. The lover speaks in imperatives, and the imperative belongs to revelation as the indicative did to creation.[49] The command is a calling forth of the beloved. The winter of enclosedness is past; now is the time for the brightness of sunshine, the budding of flowers, and the song of birds. The lover wants to see the face of his beloved and hear her voice. He compares her to a dove hidden in the cranny of the rock, an image which calls to mind Rosenzweig's statement that, "It is only, after all, in the love of God that the flower of the soul begins to grow out of the rock of the self.[50] This is the condition of revelation--the enclosed beloved must open up so that she can hear and see and become a loving soul.[51]

In the context of this dialogue of love, we are at the heart of Rosenzweig's understanding of revelation. Contrary to the nineteenth-century understanding of revelation as the cognitive making explicit of what is implicit, Rosenzweig sees the analogy of love as central.[52] In fact, the analogy of love is seen here as more than an analogy:

> Thus it is not enough that God's relationship to man is explained by the simile of the lover and the beloved. God's word must contain the relationship of lover to beloved directly, the significant, that is, without any pointing to the significate. And so we find it in the *Song of Songs.* Here it is no longer possible to see in that simile "only a simile." Here the reader seems to be confronted by the choice, either to accept the "purely human," purely sensual sense and then, admittedly, to ask himself what strange error allowed these pages to slip into God's word, or to acknowledge that the deeper meaning lodges here, precisely in the

purely sensual sense, directly and not "merely" in simile.[53]

It is the latter alternative which Rosenzweig himself chooses, and in the direct sense which he has indicate, i.e., not seeing revelation as primarily a cognitive matter which happens to be nicely illustrated by love analogies, but opting for love as the central structure of revelation.

Thus revelation is a matter, not of new knowledge, but of a new relationship in love. Just as in every deep love experience, one's world comes together in a new way and one's self is re-born and the other is re-discovered as lover so, too, in the experience of revelation the three barren elements of God, world, and the human person--all of which Rosenzweig described as isolated elements in the first section of *The Star*--emerge from themselves, belong to one another, and meet one another.[54]

Revelation re-creates the human person; warmed by God's love, the mute self comes of age as eloquent soul.[55] It is only now that a person finds the strength to exist in the face of death--Rosenzweig's preoccupation on the very next pages of *The Star*. Revelation has the knowledge that love is as strong as death. It is only the beloved soul, called from muteness to eloquence, who can sing:

Let me be a seal upon your heart
Like the seal upon your hand.
For love is fierce as death,
Passion is mighty as Sheol;
Its darts are darts of fire,
A blazing flame.
Vast floods cannot quench love,
Nor rivers drown it.
If a man offered all his wealth for love,
He would be laughed to scorn.
(The Song of Songs, 8: 6-7)

Revelation wakens something in creation which is as strong as death. This new creation is the beloved soul--what Rosenzweig calls "the unearthly in earthly life."[56]

In reflecting on Rosenzweig's central insight here, not only do we see the human person coming alive in a new way, not just as the receptacle for a "deposit of faith," but God too emerges from the dusty objectivity of the nineteenth century. He is not the God of whom Samuel Hirsch wrote: "God's sun shines and enlightens everyone and wants to waken all men to the discovery of powerful life. If the evil man wants to turn himself away from this sun, if he wants to develop without the light and warmth of this sun, the sun nevertheless goes right on shining and giving warmth. It is the evil man who has robbed himself of the principle of life which was destined for him."[57] It is precisely this kind of God whom Rosenzweig denies. "Divine love does not, like light, radiate in all directions as an essential attitude. Rather it transfixes individuals--men, nations, epochs, things--in an enigmatic transfixion."[58] God's love has an infinity of time in which to meet his creation and re-create it through the disclosure of himself as lover. God is much more the lover in pursuit of the beloved than the all-shining sun.

Rather than merely define terms and develop argument or outline thematic development chapter by chapter, the attempt has been made to plunge immediately *in medias res*, into the core experience which is the heart of Rosenzweig's entire enterprise in *The Star of Redemption*. Before coming to grips with this, one is merely dancing at the periphery; it is possible to go through all the twists and turns of Rosenzweig's dialectic of "yea" and "nay," study all the ramifications of his negative differential, examine and dissect the multiple triadic structures of the book--and be nowhere. It is equally possible for a person at prayer to be at the heart of what Rosenzweig is saying: "Prayer is the last thing achieved by revelation. . . to be able to pray: that is the greatest gift presented to the soul in revelation."[59]

It is demanding to make the kind of fundamental reorientation required by Rosenzweig; the cognitive bias is deep in philosophical history. The point of Rosenzweig's book is missed without the realization that it is not a point at all: not a piece of cognitive information, not a syllogism or thought-schema. Rosenzweig wants to move beyond cognition:

Cognition has everything, true, but only as elements, only in its pieces. Experience goes beyond the piecemeal; it was whole at every moment, but because it was always at the moment, it did not, though it was whole, have everything in any of its moments.[60]

Therein lies part of the frustration in reading and trying to understand Rosenzweig--the isolated elements, the cognitive units, the essences--these do not contain the truth. The truth is in the dialogue, in the story, in their dynamic courses.

In a similar way, one has to forego seeing the points, in order to see their configuration:

"What becomes immediately visible in revelation is neither God nor man nor world. On the contrary, God, man, and world which had been visible figures in paganism, here lose their visibility: God appears to be concealed, man secluded, the world enchanted. What does become visible is their reciprocal interaction. That which is here immediately experienced is not God, man, and world but rather creation, revelation, and redemption."[61]

Like the moving blades of a fan, the elements can no longer be seen in their individuality, but only in their interactive pattern.

In the moment when the three elements converge in experience, it is the configuration which alone is visible:

"God within himself separates into the God who creates and the God of love and mercy. Man separates into the soul beloved by God and the lover who loves his neighbor. The world separates into the existence of the creature that longs for God's creation and life that grows toward and into the kingdom of God."[62]

There is a very real sense in which revelation contains everything, because revelation is presentness; a presentness that is the context of dialogue. It is only in the presentness of revelation that one can see the disparate elements of God, world, and the human person run their courses and emerge in the configuration of a star.

CHAPTER THREE
Notes

1. Rosenzweig, *Briefe und Tagebücher*, I-2, p. 603.

2. Rosenzweig, *Briefe und Tagebücher*, I-2, p.640. This is from another letter to Rudolf Ehrenberg, sent from Kassel on July 24, 1919.

3. Rosenzweig, *Briefe und Tagebücher*, I-2, p. 645.

4. Rosenzweig, *Briefe und Tagebücher*, I-2, pp. 718-719. Translation my own.

5. This story can be read in Glatzer, *Franz Rosenzweig: His Life and Thought*, pp. 108ff.

6. Rosenzweig, *Zweistromland*, p. 139.

7. Rosenzweig, *Zweistromland*, p. 140.

8. Rosenzweig, *Zweistromland*, p. 143.

9. Glatzer, *Franz Rosenzweig: His Life and Thought*, p. 192. The original is in Rosenzweig, *Zweistromland*, p. 144.

10. Rosenzweig calls this "erfahrende Philosophie" which translates somewhat awkwardly into English.

11. Rosenzweig, *Zweistromland*, p. 152.

12. In *Das Dialogische Denken* Bernhard Casper discusses the philosophy of Buber, Ebner, and Rosenzweig. In a conversation with Rosenzweig's widow in Berlin on March 22, 1976, I was interested to learn that in her opinion it was this

Catholic priest whom she considered to be the best living interpreter of her husband's thought.

13. Rosenzweig, *Zweistromland*, p. 142.

14. Rosenzweig, *Zweistromland*, p. 150.

15. Rosenzweig, *Zweistromland*, p. 151.

16. Rosenzweig, *Zweistromland*, p. 145.

17. Rosenzweig, *Zweistromland*, p. 146. Translation my own.

18. Protology (the study of first things) and eschatology (the study of last things) serve as history's bookends. Protological motifs and images are often found again in eschatological discourse. Thus, the biblical discussion of end-time reality reflects in many ways the description of our human origin in a garden of peace and understanding.

19. Rosenzweig, Franz, *The Star of Redemption*, trans. by W. W. Hallo (New York: Holt, Rinehart & Winston, 1970), p. 175.

20. Rosenzweig, *The Star of Redemption*, p. 175.

21. Rosenzweig, *Zweistromland*, p. 153.

22. Rosenzweig, *Briefe und Tagebücher*, I-2, pp. 994-995.

23. Rosenzweig, *Zweistromland*, p. 154. The translation is from Glatzer, *Franz Rosenzweig: His Life and Thought*, p. 202.

24. Rosenzweig, *Briefe und Tagebücher*, I-2, pp. 708-709. Translation my own.

25. Rosenzweig, *Briefe und Tagebücher*, I-2, p. 717.

26. Rosenzweig, *The Star of Redemption*, p. 183.

27. Rosenzweig, *The Star of Redemption*, p. 187.

28. Rosenzweig, *The Star of Redemption*, p. 188.

29. Rosenzweig, *Briefe und Tagebücher*, I-1, p. 426.

30. Rosenzweig, *Zweistromland*, pp. 801-815.

31. Rosenzweig, *Zweistromland*, p. 804.   Translation my own.

32. Rosenzweig, *Zweistromland*, p. 804.   Translation my own.

33. Rosenzweig, *The Star of Redemption*, p. 177.

34. Rosenzweig, *The Star of Redemption*, p. 176.

35. Rosenzweig, *The Star of Redemption*, p. 176.

36. Rosenzweig, *The Star of Redemption*, p. 177.

37. Rosenzweig, *On Jewish Learning*, p. 166.

38. Rosenzweig, *On Jewish Learning*, p. 113.

39. Rosenzweig, *Briefe und Tagebücher*, I-2, p. 951.

40. Rosenzweig, *Briefe und Tagebücher*, I-2, p. 951. Translation my own.

41. Rosenzweig, *On Jewish Learning*, p. 118.

42. Rosenzweig, *On Jewish Learning*, p. 118.

43. Rosenzweig, *Briefe und Tagebücher*, I-2, p. 762. Translation my own.

44. Rosenzweig, *Briefe und Tagebücher*, I-2, p. 762. Translation my own.

45. Rosenzweig, *The Star of Redemption*, p. 181.

46. Rosenzweig, *The Star of Redemption*, p. 180.

47. Rosenzweig, *The Star of Redemption*, p. 202.

48. Rosenzweig, *The Star of Redemption*, p. 423.

49. Rosenzweig, *The Star of Redemption*, p. 186.

50. Rosenzweig, *The Star of Redemption*, p. 169.

51. Rosenzweig, *The Star of Redemption*, p. 167.

52. Rosenzweig, *The Star of Redemption*, p. 199.

53. Rosenzweig, *The Star of Redemption*, p. 199.

54. Rosenzweig, *The Star of Redemption*, p. 115.

55. Rosenzweig, *The Star of Redemption*, p. 198.

56. Rosenzweig, *The Star of Redemption*, p. 326. Stephane Moses offers a provocative interpretation of Rosenzweig's understanding of revelation in his diary entries of 1922. Moses argues that Rosenzweig moves to an increasingly mystical view of revelation, less bound to the historical forms of Judaism and Christianity. His article, "Franz Rosenzweig in Perspective: Reflections on his last Diaries" appears on pp. 185-201 of *The Philosophy of Franz Rosenzweig* (Hanover, NH: University Press of New England, 1988), edited by Paul Mendes-Flohr.

57. Samuel Hirsch, *Die Humanität als Religion* (Trier: Troschel, 1854), p. 110. Translation my own.

58. Rosenzweig, *The Star of Redemption*, p. 164.

59. Rosenzweig, *The Star of Redemption*, p. 184.

60. Rosenzweig, *The Star of Redemption*, p. 391.

61. Rosenzweig, *The Star of Redemption*, p. 391.

62. Rosenzweig, *The Star of Redemption*, p. 306.

CHAPTER FOUR

THE TWO RELIGIONS OF REVELATION

A JOURNEY OF DISCOVERY

It is Rosenzweig's clear conviction that there are two valid religions of revelation: Judaism and Christianity. Our investigation of Rosenzweig's thought through the lens of his revelational theology has given us the theoretical underpinning of this conviction. For if revelation were totally propositional, then two faith communities differing in credal statements could not simultaneously be valid. But a dialogical model of revelation in a pre-propositional or trans-propositional matrix does indeed allow for the possibility of more than one authentic expression of revealed truth.

How do these two religions of revelation relate to each other? Where do they agree and disagree? How do they challenge, complement, and corroborate each other? These are the questions now to be addressed. Two areas of the Rosenzweig material relevant to these questions are readily available to the English-speaking reader: *The Star of Redemption* and Rosenzweig's correspondence with Rosenstock.[1]

One important source remains largely unavailable to the English-language reader, and until 1979, only partially available to the German-language reader; namely, Rosenzweig's extensive correspondence with Hans Ehrenberg.[2] Although utilizing the entire Rosenzweig corpus, our focus in this chapter will be on this exchange of letters. Other than its relative inaccessibility until recent years, is there any other

83

compelling reason for selecting this material? I believe there is. Rosenzweig's wife told me in my 1976 interview with her that no one had better understood her husband's thought than Hans Ehrenberg; thus Hans was one of Franz's earliest and most authoritative interpreters. Furthermore, Hans went on to receive formal training as a Protestant minister; he was not only a Christian but a man destined to become a professional theologian, an articulate exponent of Christian faith.

Much is made of Rosenzweig's correspondence with Rosenstock; its importance is incontrovertible. It could well be argued, however, that an English edition of Rosenzweig's exchange of letters with Hans Ehrenberg could make an even greater contribution to Jewish--Christian dialogue.[3]   Why?   Because Franz himself refers to a freedom in dialogue with Hans that he finds lacking in his exchanges with Eugen.   Rosenzweig writes Ehrenberg in 1918:

> You are certainly not going to be able to talk easily with Rosenstock. He has too little ability to think inside another person and too much of a tendency to think against him. That's the shadow side of his vitality. He forces every discussion into the form of a duel; whereas, a good discussion has the basic form of a journey of discovery and only becomes a duel when it just happens. But he totally lacks this element of a journey of discovery. And so his partner in dialogue must work all the harder to bring this element into the discussion. Otherwise it all remains fruitless.[4]

Rosenzweig's correspondence with Rosenstock was fruitful, but his correspondence with Hans Ehrenberg is less of a duel and much more a true journey of discovery.

"Journey of discovery" offers a telling insight into the deeper nature of dialogue. First of all, dialogue is an adventure, a voyage, a process, a moving dynamic; dialogue demands more than a static reshuffling of staid categories and definitions. Secondly, dialogue entails discovery; one has to be ready for surprises. There can be no canned scripts or cue cards or answers in the back of the book. The partners in dialogue must prepare themselves for a journey of unscheduled events. The feel for this kind of journey of discovery is precisely what Rosenzweig found lacking in Rosenstock, but it is clear that he enjoyed this kind of atmosphere in his extensive communication with Hans Ehrenberg.

Franz and Hans were related. Born in 1883, Hans was three years his cousin's senior.[5] Hans converted to Christianity, was ordained a minister, escaped Nazi Germany to England, and returned to post-war Germany where he remained until his death in 1958.

Our concern with the correspondence is in terms of the light it throws on Rosenzweig's understanding of the relationship of Judaism and Christianity. Hans did what Franz had once contemplated but never initiated; he converted to Christianity. Franz became what Hans had never been, a religiously committed Jew. So close to each other in age, culture, and background, the different shapes their lives assumed somehow became all the more significant. Let us pick up the relationship in terms of an event which came to be a bone of contention between Franz and his parents, the announcement of Hans' conversion to Christianity.

In a letter of April 29, 1918, Franz discusses with Hans the rhythm of their relationship. He notes a period of mutual alienation which began in 1910 and which he now sees as ending; this 1910 date coincides with Hans Ehrenberg's baptism as a Christian. Although Rosenzweig argued with his parents in defense of his cousin's decision,[6] it might well be that the issue was not so easily resolved--at least not within Franz's unconscious. Rosenzweig's 1913 decision to remain a Jew illustrates the level of personal turmoil which Ehrenberg's decision undoubtedly touched. Let us examine this important letter more closely:

I have nothing to forgive you, for you personally have never hurt me. You are less rough than you think. I perceived our drifting apart as fate, as one of those necessities of life, first for you, soon afterwards for me as well. I know well that I have hurt you. And yet I find that in friendship it is no more necessary to ask forgiveness for the bad things we do than to say thanks for the good. Just as it's not necessary to ask oneself for forgiveness or to thank oneself. In a relationship like ours, these kinds of feelings should be addressed to another party.

I can only speak for the past and for the present. But I know that our friendship is now experiencing a phase of opposition just as prior to 1910 it was in a phase of conjunction. But friendship doesn't change on this account. Friendship is actually indestructible. Even friendships torn totally apart still remain friendships. The comet which has once come through my solar system and crossed my path will someday once again be visible, even if that's only after a long time. And our relationship cannot be described in terms of unstable comets but is thoroughly planetary.

I had, however, forgotten that bit of our "shared (planetary) rotation" at . . .'s wedding. But that's not simply a question of age or youth. Our friendship was always so anchored in objectivity (naturally not every man's objectivity but an objectivity shared only by us) that its future phases will also have something more than what we would really like, something lying outside the control of our good will. Like you I, too, have the feeling that the period of being in opposition is at an end. But as yet I don't see in the least the path that is now before us. If we should come again into conjunction--you can count on that--we would walk again with each other in our 30s and be just as much in love as we were in our 20s. At least with people like us there is no question of age. But as I said, I sense a change but I don't see how it is happening.[7]

The letter manifests a frankness which characterizes Rosenzweig's correspondence with Ehrenberg. At the same time, a great tenderness and intimacy permeate the letter, revealing the depth of the relationship;　they were too close to be politely civil. There were indeed storms along the way of their mutual journey of discovery, days of fog and darkness. The relationship was maintained, however, through all the vicissitudes of travel;　or, to use Rosenzweig's image, they were destined to orbit together as sister planets, even though there were periods when their paths held them apart.　　One such period was undoubtedly 1910-1918, a time when their relationship had to adjust to the reciprocal shock of Ehrenberg's conversion to Christianity and Rosenzweig's new-found connection to his Jewishness.

The letter would be valuable for its insights into friendship alone, but it also illustrates for us the depth of trust from which real dialogue must proceed. Honest Jewish-Christian dialogue requires a certain toughness that moves beyond mere politeness and allows for honest disagreement, even alienation and feelings of estrangement.　A Christian veneer of philosemitism, a Jewish sentimentality for all things Christian--these attitudes open no door of true dialogue.

Rosenzweig writes Ehrenberg on December 26, 1917.　This is during the time which he refers to as their "opposition period" before they came again into conjunction after 1918.　We sense the strength, even the vehemence, with which Rosenzweig wants to stress their differences as Jew and Christian;　dialogue cannot begin with any blurring of distinctions.　Rosenzweig insists that through his conversion to Christianity,

Ehrenberg has lost all access to the inner side of Judaism. The letter is severe, acerbic, even sarcastic. From a discussion of the arts, the letter makes an abrupt change to a religious agenda:

Regarding the human person, our religions are *not* dissimilar, since Christianity too teaches love of the neighbor.[8] And with this literary bridge I should thereby be arriving at your theme. Dear Hans, neighborly-loved Hans, we simply can't talk about it[9]--at least not as long as you still base any kind of consciousness of a closer knowledge or relevance or even interest in "Jewish questions" on your former, state-notarized membership in the Jewish faith. You just don't have that. You can study your way through mountains of "new" and "old" Jewish literature and you won't be one finger's width closer to it. Take, for example, your inquisitional questions about my position on the "direction" of the Hasidic tale. You are undoubtedly waiting for a yes or no and when I tell you neither yes nor no you'll take it as an evasion. The tale in question is really a *joke*! But if, instead of admitting that you just do not understand or don't believe me, you would say, "Damn, that is really true!", then I have to turn around in desperation and say that it is *not* a joke.

If you could even once use the word *nebbish*[10] correctly and not always in a situation where it would never occur to any Jew to use it or if you could ever understand *one* "Jewish joke" at any level like a Jew, which in this case means to understand it like one who loves, and not like a Christian, which in this case means like one who hates and despises. But that is something you will never be able to do, no matter how much you might like to do it. Jewish piety and Jewish humor live in the same organ, the Jewish heart, and no road leads to that place from foreign brains or foreign hearts.[11] Just remain with the old master Hegel (who by the way really took the same political and philosophical stand towards Judaism as you--namely liberal politically and negative philosophically) and don't acknowledge an existence without existence--namely, the essence of an existence without existence; if you acknowledged it you would immediately give it existence; through your not being able to acknowledge it you thereby help it precisely to conserve its own existence. This is also why I can't listen to your judgment about whether my Judaism is Judaism. The dumbest Jewish boy has more right (and ability) for this kind of judgment than you. You may judge my utterances, productions, politics, history, theology as "too Jewish" or "unacceptably Jewish" or "absolutely un-Jewish" or "Christian" or "too Christian" (a comical list)-- that is your right and that is where I will always be attentive in listening to you. But "not Jewish enough"--no, that's a judgment not to be made by *you*.[12]

This is not so much a letter as an artillery barrage; it is hard to imagine Hans easily recovering from such an attack. Rosenzweig's position is exaggerated but not without purpose; he refuses to leave his cousin one shred of his former Jewish identity, insisting that baptism has washed away every trace of his Jewishness. There can be no Jewish Christians, not Hans or Rudolf Ehrenberg, not Eugen Rosenstock. It is an either-or proposition: either Jewish or Christian.

This is a theme we will encounter again in this correspondence. In an environment so largely Christian, it is imperative for Rosenzweig to mark out and protect that space which is totally and exclusively Jewish. This is not contrary to dialogue but in a very real sense a prerequisite; Jews and Christians cannot understand themselves and each other if they are attempting to live within a so-called Judeo-Christian amalgam.[13]

JOHANNINE CHRISTIANITY

The importance of this sharp delineation of Judaism and Christianity as a *sine qua non* of genuine dialogue again receives explicit mention in another letter to Ehrenberg. Earlier, Rosenzweig had said that they could not speak on the subject of religion precisely because Ehrenberg was trying to present himself as both Jew and Christian. Now Rosenzweig recognizes that a change has taken place.

> . . . you have this time admitted something very important and thereby made the discussion first really possible (even necessary, though personally it is still not important for me). You did this precisely because you finally stated that your Jewish Christianity is not outside of Judaism and Christianity but a Christian denomination, a new epoch of church history. And so we come out again at the Johannine epoch. We won't argue about the 19th century, whether you want to define the Idealists as the first fathers of the new church, Schopenhauer and Nietzsche as its first great heretics and Freemasonry as its organization or whether you would rather first put the beginning today and understand the whole 19th century from the Idealists on as the prelude to this today, that is really not important. The main thing is that Catholicism and Protestantism are old denominations and something new is on the scene today. It's been clear to me for a long time that this new

phenomenon has strong ties to Judaism (just as the Catholic church from 313 had to the northern peoples and the Protestant and the Counter-Reformation churches had to classical antiquity). I've expressed myself on this point before--first around 1909 or 1911 and quite definitely in recent years. Each of these epochs of ecclesiastical history has been accompanied by an event in world history: the emigration of the northern peoples goes with the Catholic period; the Renaissance goes with the Protestant phase; the emancipation of the Jews belongs with the Johannine epoch. I already admitted to you on the trip from Jüterbog to Alteslager the striking similarity of our developing thoughts on this matter, even though we had no influence on each other in this regard.

Now that you have let go of your claim to some type of intermediate position between Judaism and Christianity and have declared yourself as totally Christian, a shared platform for speaking with each other is established. You may call the new denomination Jewish Christianity but then, for the sake of clarity, you should name the two old denominations Teutonic Christianity[14] and pagan Christianity. Those really would not be bad names. They would express the *imperishability* of both old *churches*. For the European world--even in terms of the current re-mapping of Europe--[15] does not cease to be the field of Christianity. By the same token, the pre-Christian world collectively understood as "classical antiquity" does not cease to be the inner opposition to the flow of Christianity. And, at the same time, these two names point to the *pastness* of both old *epochs* of ecclesiastical history. For the Teutonizing of Christianity, not of course the Christianizing of the Teutons, is complete with

1517, just as the Platonizing of Christianity, not the Christianizing of Plato, is complete with "1800." Thirdly, with the word 'Jewish Christianity' what is expressed is that the Johannine epoch can have no end *in* history. For not only the Christianizing of the Jews but also the Judaising of Christianity can reach no completion in history, since with this completion history would also have reached its completion, something which Paul saw quite correctly. The accomplished Judaising of Christianity means the exclusion of Christ. Or to put this another way, the year zero has a temporal relationship to the years before and after zero, but it has only an eternal relationship to eternity. That is why Christianity first reaches its absoluteness as Jewish Christianity, as Johannine Christianity.

Its absoluteness--for "the real dogma of Christianity" states, 'I, the *one sent*, am the Way, the Truth, and the Life' and that turns the absoluteness of Christianity into an absoluteness in time, but into a relativity vis-a-vis eternity. If the "one sent" can say: 'I am the Way' then God can no longer say it. Then all that can still be said of God is that he is Love. So it remains for Judaism to make the claim that God is the *Truth* and love is only his *attribute* (and as such his commandment) but not his *essence*.

And here I think I'm precisely at the point of indicating where it is that the Jew and the Christian stand in opposition (you probably see already with how much correctness and incorrectness) and reproach each other with being respectively godless or loveless. It is no distortion of Christianity, as you think, to place God at the last end, so long as Christianity adheres to the sentence, "I am the Way," etc. as its essential dogma, and so

forever, as long as there remains no place for
the living God. Granted there's place for God's
aliveness, all the more so. This is where I
come to something where you have
misunderstood me. I have not claimed of
Judaism that it covers itself with another
truth outside of itself. I grant you completely
the this-worldly, nonvitality of Judaism. I
thought that you knew that. Judaism is alive
only insofar as it is with God. It is only when
the world is also with God that Judaism will
be alive in the world as well. That is again,
of course, outside of history.

Possessing the real truth, Judaism is
allowed to be unconcerned about reality. But
the Christian, out of love for the truth, must
not shut himself off from reality. It's quite
clear there are two who delay the coming of
the kingdom of God: the Jew who involves
himself with reality more than he should and
the Christian who involves himself less with it
than he can.[16]

This letter is a veritable gold mine of theological
material relevant to Jewish-Christian dialogue. What
are these three kinds of Christianity to which
Rosenzweig refers? What, especially, is the nature of
this third phase of Christianity which Rosenzweig
identifies both as Johannine and as Jewish
Christianity? What is the theological significance of the
Christian dogma of Jesus as the Way, the Truth, and
the Life? What does Rosenzweig see as the
complementary roles the two faith communities play
vis-a-vis history and eternity?

The conception of three stages in Christian history
stems from Schelling.[17] The earliest phase, Petrine
Christianity, is identified with the Roman Church and
is also called "pagan Christianity" in this letter.
Protestantism or Pauline Christianity signifies the
triumph of the Teutonic genius and culminates with

Luther's Reformation in 1517. The Johannine epoch of Christianity began, according to Rosenzweig, with the events following the French Revolution.[18]

The reference to 1800 in the letter has to do with the connections of the Renaissance or classical antiquity to the second phase of church history, both in its Protestant and Counter-Reformation forms. In an earlier letter to Ehrenberg, Rosenzweig wrote: "The pre-Christian knowledge was accepted by the Church around 1500, but was finally digested by the Church around 1800. Since 1800 the Greeks are neither a power nor a burden."[19] In the same letter Rosenzweig indicates that this digestion of Greek knowledge was accomplished by Hegel who is, therefore the last of the philosophers.[20]

The emancipation of the Jews accompanies the third epoch of Christianity, its Johannine phase. The emergence of Jews from the ghetto enabled Judaism to exert a new influence on Christian theology. Rosenzweig's insight that the Greek influence (which culminated in Hegel) would decline in its impact on Christian theology and that the Jewish--and therefore biblical--influence would increase, has proved astonishingly perspicacious. It remains to be seen whether he is also accurate in maintaining that this period could not end within history but only with history.

Johannine Christianity endures to the end of history; this means that Judaism's role vis-a'-vis Christianity must likewise endure, since Johannine Christianity is also Jewish Christianity. During this period, Judaism must manifest the Absolute, just as Christianity radiates the Relative. And why is this? Because of the relationship of Christianity to Christ. The Christian centering in Christ constitutes both its glory and its limitation. If Christ is Christianity's truth, then God (the Father in the Christian Trinity) cannot claim that identical position.

God, in some sense, must wait until the end. The other side of that statement is that when God again becomes central, Christ will be displaced. Rosenzweig assures Ehrenberg that he should not be disturbed by that because St. Paul rightly understood that same logic. Rosenzweig expands on this point in *The Star* where he writes:

> The first theologian of the new religion teaches that the Son, when once all will have submitted to him, will turn over his dominion to the Father, and then God will be all in all. But one can see at once that this is a theologism. For Christian piety it is meaningless. It depicts a distant, far distant future. It deals with the last things by explicitly depriving them of all influence on time. For the dominion belongs to the Son, as yet and for all time, and God is not all-in-all.[21]

The Christocentric character of Christianity, which is essential to it, renders it incapable of being simultaneously theocentric. Thus from the viewpoint of Judaism it remains in some sense godless. On the other hand, the love of God manifested in Christ is so vibrantly incarnate for Christianity that Judaism seems by comparison loveless.

This point finds illustration in the respective calendars of the two communities. As Rosenzweig points out in this letter, the Christian calendar has a year zero (signifying the birth of Christ) and all history translates into B.C. or A.D. This locates the Christian differently in history from the Jew whose calendar is dated from creation; Judaism recognizes no temporal interruption in its orientation to eternity.

Rosenzweig's language about the Jew not being in history, not being in the world, not having to be concerned about reality, can be misleading. It has to do with a theological structure indicated by his comment on the calendar. Rosenzweig claims the Jew exists in a free field from eternity to eternity, from creation to the kingdom of God; there is no human person or event which interrupts this flow. Nothing relative--neither Abraham nor Moses, neither the crossing of the Red Sea nor the giving of the Torah--infringes on the claim of the Absolute. Only God is God. The claim of God is absolute, calling the Jew to live on the other side of history.

THE INTERIM KINGDOM

Christianity, according to Rosenzweig, has absolutized the relative in two ways. The first of these lies in its Christology and finds expression in: the Christian Testament (especially John, the fourth and last of the canonical gospels), the dogma of Christ's divinity, and the Christian calendar with its before and after the birth of Christ. The humanity of Jesus and the temporal nature of his messiahship are overlooked because of the emphasis on his divinity. The second way in which Christianity absolutizes the relative is in terms of its understanding of the interim kingdom (*Zwischenreich*), the subject of Rosenzweig's May 19, 1918 letter to his cousin:

Dear Hans, regarding your historical problem, you must first of all hold that immortality was already known to the pagans. What was new and became a stumbling block to the pagan world was not the immortality of the soul but the resurrection of the *body*. You can already see that with Augustine, even better in Tertullian (*De Anima, De Resurrectione Carnis*).[22] On the whole, Idealism was a pagan invention. Revelation is what rescues matter threatened on all sides by the Idealistic decay and reinstates it in its rightful place against spirit--within the spirit it is soul against spirit, taken further it is time against timelessness, space against concept etc., etc. So it comes about that the resurrection, deeply embedded in reality and tied to the "flesh" and the course of world history, replaces the spiritual, all too spiritual immortality. What an obscenity for the Platonists! But truthfully, what a strengthening of reality against Plato. I cannot disown my body, not there and therefore not here, this body, my body, both here and there. I cannot give myself airs about one part of my being and turn against another part of my being. This most proper escape is blocked for me. I am totally myself; it is as a totality that I'll be judged. And this world in which I live is not an alien one, whose destiny does not touch my bliss. Rather, the arrival of my true happiness depends on the fulfillment of that destiny. The "immortality in every moment" of Schleiermacher and Fichte is an empty phrase. Yet every time must be fulfilled so that the fruit of eternity might ripen. And this is true of revelation in its origin and entrance into the world. And now this new 'materialistic' concept of happiness is beginning (most prominently of course in Christianity but paralleled in Judaism as well) to put some color into the thin-spirited ones we came upon earlier. Nevertheless, it remains always secondary, provisional, needing fulfillment. Reward and punishment retain something preliminary. The whole blessedness is really only a mirror of the interim kingdom. This is how Dante presents it, for his poem really only takes place in the interim kingdom and has practically forgotten eschatology, at least in the practical/aesthetic order. Naturally, theoretical afterthoughts remain for him too. Perhaps there was only one time when a word was spoken (and perhaps it was the only time when it could have been spoken) in which the

two concepts of happiness were completely
blended together; namely, the 'today you will
be with me in Paradise.' (Luke 23:43) It's
precisely with this verse that you can see the
motive from which Christianity--though it
thoroughly shatters the premises of that
verse--must now to some degree let this
disappointed thief on the cross nevertheless
belatedly be right. And he must be allowed
'today' to come at least into a provisional
Paradise, that heaven about which, just as
much as about the earth, it was written that it
will 'pass away' and God will create a new
heaven and a new earth (Isaiah 65:17; Peter
3:13; Revelation 21:1). But as we said, *this*
happiness remains secondary, a playground of
superstition, at least a place where faith and
superstition are found together, the
superstition about the life of this eon, the faith
about the perfect happiness of the coming
world. The picture mingles the aftertaste of
the one and the foretaste of the other. It is
characteristic of Christianity precisely as the
religion of the interim kingdom that it devotes
relatively so much power to this concept of
happiness. Here, too, Christianity is the
legitimate imitator of paganism, whose
inheritance it entered, granted in order that it
might reconstruct it, in the sense which I
spoke of earlier. In Judaism this concept has
remained strong in the folklore traditions and
rarely shows up in the theological realm.[23]

Rosenzweig first addresses the question of the
interim kingdom in terms of conflicting notions of
after-life. He has already isolated what he considers a
general tendency in Christianity to absolutize the
relative, to bring what is at the end of history into
history. This was the principal direction of his
comments on the calendar and christological dogmas.

Perhaps this orientation can already be discerned in the synoptic gospel accounts of the core content of Jesus' preaching; namely, that the reign of God is near, at hand, in our midst. Is this same tendency to be found in Christian considerations of life after death and the meaning of final beatitude? Rosenzweig answers in the affirmative.

Rosenzweig begins the letter by contrasting the pagan notions of immortality of the soul with the traditional Jewish and Christian teaching of the resurrection of the body. The theology stems, of course, from the original Hebrew-language mindset which views the human person holistically, never having developed the Platonic body/soul dualism which was even more deeply entrenched in Western consciousness through Descartes and the advent of modern philosophy. Rosenzweig gives powerful expression to this nondualistic philosophical anthropology.

Rejecting the separation of the human person into discrete body and soul entities, Rosenzweig likewise denies the possibility of separating the human person from the world. In the dualistic context, nonidentification with one's bodiliness is generally accomplished by a similar nonidentification with earthly existence; in such a context, abstention from everything material becomes synonymous with virtue; this is the path of holy abstinence. Rosenzweig, on the other hand, adheres to the spirituality of blessed participation which is rooted in the biblical perspective of a good creation and a holistic human reality.

The model of holy abstinence can best be understood through a vertical diagram in which one approaches the Divine through a progressive separation from the human. Abstinence from sexual activity, minimal speaking, sleeping, eating and drinking--these become primary virtues. The model of blessed participation, on the other hand, suggests a horizontal diagram. Every blessing includes both the recognition of the transcendent mystery (Blessed are You, Lord God, King of the Universe) and the reference to a created reality: bread or wine, the celebration of the newlywed couple, children. The participation in the created reality within a covenanted context is constitutive of this path of holiness.

How do these ideas affect one's understanding of final blessedness? If the material world is evil and we are essentially composed of two distinct entities, and if one of those entities is intrinsically related to the evil material world, then the path of final blessedness is clear. The spiritual principle (the soul) must be freed from material reality both in its particular form (the body) and in its universal manifestation (the world). This, of course, makes this blessedness immediately attainable either through death or through the spiritual identification with this higher realm. This notion of spiritual bliss is unrelated to the body and the course of world history; it is, in other words, atemporal.

The affirmation of embeddedness in the created world and a nondualistic self-identity lead to another concept of final blessedness which is related to bodiliness and contingent on the fulfillment of the world. This view of the final beatitude is not available in the here and now but must be the ripe fruit of all creation reaching its fullness. Once again, then, we see Rosenzweig's rejection of the principle of taking something which is beyond history--in this case, final blessedness--and making it available in the present order of history.

Which concept of celestial bliss belongs to Christianity? Christian doctrine proclaims the enfleshment of God in Jesus and his bodily resurrection; furthermore, Christianity preserves the Hebrew scriptures as its own Old Testament. Should not its witness, then, be the same as Judaism's? What Rosenzweig reminds us of here is that Christianity entered into the inheritance of the pagan world. The Hellenistic thinkers who converted to Christianity did not lose their philosophical mind-set in the baptismal pool. On the contrary, the message of salvation was translated into their language and processed in their categories. Christianity was hellenized from its early centuries up to the time of Hegel. The process, however, was never able to be completed, precisely because of the Hebraic heritage which could never be totally eradicated. In this final Johannine age of Christian history, the Jewish tradition will work actively in Christian thought and a more materialistic theology of final blessedness will, as Rosenzweig expresses it, put some color in the paler version of beatitude which formerly held sway in Christian ideology.[24]

Rosenzweig's use of the Lucan passage about the "good thief" is instructive; here he sees a blending of the two traditions. Jesus' promise of a Paradise *today* must, for Rosenzweig, relate to the interim kingdom. The final reign of God is not available in this "today." On the other hand, as a messianic figure, Jesus does point to the culminating *today* of God's reign. This kind of blending is essential to Christian theology, but Rosenzweig sees it as present to Judaism only in its folklore tradition.

Rosenzweig continues his letter to his cousin on the following day, May 11, 1918:

So much for openers. For the rest, you seem unfortunately to have come back again to that unacceptable standpoint which you seemed to have freed yourself from in your earlier letter. I see that I have to explain to you the Jewish relationship to the "interim kingdom" from a somewhat closer range (therefore, somewhat dialectically). I have already written you regarding the fact that it is not enough that the Christian lives from the beginning of the interim kingdom and the Jew lives from its end. Therefore, to be more exact: the Christian relationship to the interim kingdom is one of affirmation; the Jewish relationship is one of negation. What will be affirmed or denied? The interim. How does one affirm an interim? By positing the beginning as positive, as having been, and the end as negative, as not yet having been. So this is not necessarily your personal relationship to the interim kingdom but the Christian relationship in general. The positive is always what is obvious, at least at first. So too in this case it is the affirmation of the beginning which determines the concept, which posits it, which makes it the thesis. And only the dialectic of development can bring the negative part as well to an independent significance. Going on with our questioning: how does one negate an interim? Or, more precisely, how do you express in terms of an interim that something is not an interim? (This is a problem which has a very striking analogy; namely, the concept of the irrational number.) So how does one deny an interim in this way? Insofar as one posits the beginning as negative, as not yet existing, and the end as positive, as already existing. So the beginning and end are in fact not reversed but revalued. And here you have Judaism. The beginning of the interim kingdom, the coming of the messiah, has not yet happened; the end, the kingdom of God, has already begun, is already there, is already given today for every Jew in the unmediated, definitive relationship to God Himself, in the daily "taking on oneself the yoke of the kingdom of heaven" through the fulfilling of the Law.[25]

Finally, I need to say "thank you" for the first time in our agrument since last June. For this is where you have finally worked on me maieutically. You have helped me to bring to light a very crucial formulation, a basic paradox through which all the contradictions in my material probably fall into place. The

details of this can be of no interest to you,
because the whole material is first of all
unknown to you and, secondly, even if it were
known, there is no urgency for you, while for
me it is precisely *the* priority, what is forcing
me to think. Also, I naturally do not have an
overview at this time (the egg was just laid) of
all the details; I'm only on their track. The
clear formulation of the two basic facts of
Jewish consciousness are going to have to
suffice for you; namely, the consciousness of
the messiah who has not yet come and of the
kingdom of God which is already a reality.
Both of these have a common and necessary
dependence from the Jewish standpoint on the
denial of the Christian interim kingdom. From
the mathematical analogy you can see
immediately the way Judaism looks from the
viewpoint of Christianity. What is the meaning of the irrational numbers for the rational
number? For the rational numbers, the end-
less, and in every direction eternally un-
reachable, limit can be something eternally
unlikely, though certainly always true. It's
first in the irrational number that this limit of
the rational realm of numbers strikes against
each of its individual points (those solid, count-
able, actual numbers) and frees the rational
realm of numbers from the linear abstractness
and uncertainty of one-dimensionality to a
spatial totality and thereby to certain reality.
The infinite is as infinitesimal number the
secret driving force, always invisible, of the
"visible" reality of the rational number. As
irrational number, however, it will be manifest,
visible and yet always strange: a number and
yet not a number; one could almost say an
"unnumber" if the Berlin Academy had not
forbidden such a Germanization. The world of
numbers first comes full circle with the

un-number, the really visible un-numbers, not already with the visible effective primordial numbers, the infinitesimal. If you did not know who the un-*person* is, you could discern it everyday in the newspapers.[26]

The long letter continues but the material most pertinent to our topic is in this section. The letter was written while Rosenzweig was participating in an officers' training course in Rembertow near Warsaw. This time falls between the writing of the nucleus of *The Star of Redemption* in October 1917 and the beginning of the writing of the full text in August 1918 when he is back on the Balkan front. Many of the references in the letter to the urgent and pressing task at hand undoubtedly refer to the whole larger project of *The Star.*

Rosenzweig's references to the maieutic (midwifing) effect of his cousin on him has to do with Ehrenberg's eliciting or evoking from him a fundamental paradox which provides him with an organizing principle for all the apparent contradictions in his material. What is this principle? It is clearly the positive and generative potential of the apparently negative. Historically, this is rooted in the cultural image of the Jew and Judaism in European society.

In the sister cathedrals of Strassbourg and Freiburg one can still see today, as Rosenzweig did in the early years of this century, the paired statues of church and synagogue. The church, depicted as a queen, gazes clear-eyed into the world which is her realm. But the synagogue, blindfolded and with broken staff, stands alienated in a foreign environment. Instead of decrying this anti-Jewish caricature, Rosenzweig accepts it as the starting point of his theology of Judaism.

The mathematical analogy developed in this letter has to do with rational and irrational numbers. An irrational number (like the square root of 2) is expressed as a nonterminating, non-repeating decimal.

Rosenzweig remarks that such a number seems almost like an un-number. And yet this represents the Jew who necessarily appears in Christian Europe as an un-person.[27]

Rosenzweig's stroke of genius, (one which he here attributes to his correspondence with Ehrenberg) is to appreciate the positive formulation of the apparent negative which is, nevertheless, not nothing. In other words, the unending decimal progression of the irrational numbers, though scandalous from the viewpoint of complete integers, provides a connection with infinity. Furthermore, these irrational numbers are necessary for the complete set of numbers.

In his introduction to the *The Star of Redemption*, Rosenzweig makes a similar point about the formation of the differential in calculus. Newton's "flexion" is infinitesimal and yet it too is not nothing; instead, it is generative of something. As Rosenzweig writes, "It is a Nought which points to an Aught, its Aught; at the same time it is an Aught that still slumbers in the lap of the Nought."[28] This becomes a crucial principle of development in the early part of *The Star* and may well contain Rosenzweig's quintessential insight into the relationship of Judaism and Christianity.

The brilliance of this tack lies in the fact that it accepts the opponent's definition of terms. It launches no attack where it is most expected; namely, against the anti-Jewish caricature of the synagogue and of the people whose only real identity seems to consist in denying the messianic reality which Christianity proclaims. Rosenzweig accepts the terms. Judaism is indeed blind to the realm which Christianity claims; it is without power in the interim kingdom where Christianity's attention is focused. And it does indeed deny the messianic present which Christianity affirms.

For Rosenzweig, Judaism and Christianity are both true religions but with differing perspectives irresolvedly opposed until the end of human history and with complementary functions deriving precisely from their irreconcilable differences. Like a rational number,

Christianity can point to something complete, achieved, found. Judaism, like the endlessly progressing decimal series, seems frustratingly unfinished; and yet that very lack of completion is a kind of infinity. In some sense, the irrational number is already connected with infinity; at the same time, the nonterminating decimal series is an affront and challenge to the vaunted completeness of the rational numbers. The complete set of numbers requires both, much as God's providence calls both covenantal communities into existence.

True Religion

A natural corollary of this position is the inappropriateness of the proselytizing of Jews by Christians. Such missionary activity negates the dual covenantal reality and represents a return to the earlier "replacement theology" which had characterized Christianity for most of its two thousand-year existence but which was now itself to be replaced in the emerging Johannine phase of Christianity.

In a letter of April 21, 1918 Rosenzweig writes:

I don't really recognize the distinction you're making between a religious role Christianity played for me earlier (the winter of 1913-1914) and now. Then as today I contend that: outside the church there is no salvation, except for Jews who abide in their religion.[29] This sentence is not as original as you think. At any rate, a Christian too could have said this sentence without in the least "judaizing" his religion.[30] Keep in mind, of course, that in the case of the pagans, too, we cannot simply let them roast. Somehow we have to do what Dante did in his *Inferno* where he set aside a special Elysium for them. But whoever does that is not therefore a pagan Christian or a pagan Jew. Just as I in no way perceive these viewpoints as religion but as philosophy so, too, am I unable to see your "Christian Judaism" as religion, though it touches very closely what I call my "philosophy." I just cannot understand how you can "live and die" with something like this. I accept it as truth and yet people cannot "live and die" for truth but only *reality*. What is your *reality*, the basis on which you operate? Jesus or God? If you hold that Jesus is the messiah and know yourself to belong to the interim kingdom, then God is just truth for you and Jesus alone is reality. And then you are simply a Christian, without any modifiers. And a minimum of Christology suffices for that, less than you have, much less. For me, only God is reality. I belong to the interim kingdom only because of the coercion of nature (which equals history there)--this is not my own free choice. Jesus belongs to the interim kingdom. Whether he was the messiah is something which will be proved when the messiah comes. Right now he is as problematic for me as the whole interim kingdom itself. What is certain for me is only God and His kingdom, not the interim kingdom.

And so it is that I am a Jew and you are--a Christian. How much of a Christian is your business. But the fact that you are a Christian is clear to me, and insofar as your concerns are mine, too, precisely because you are my friend, the matter of "how much" of a Christian you are concerns me too. I believe that I've made myself sufficiently clear.[31]

Some might doubt that Rosenzweig is ever "sufficiently clear" but he has made several important points in this letter. Interesting is his distinction between religion and mere philosophy; something can be true without evoking from us the conviction to live

and die for it. Religion, for Rosenzweig, must be
something on which one is willing to stake one's life.
Religion is derived from the ultimate existential concern
in each person where he or she lives most
authentically, with the most "life and death" intensity.
Rosenzweig asserts that what is finally and
convincingly real for the Jew is God and God's
kingdom; but what grasps the Christian as most real
is Christ and the interim kingdom, this present course
of sacred history. This constitutes an irreconcilable
difference in their articulated faith and spirituality.
And yet both religions are part of God's salvational
plan and providence; both covenantal communities
grasp a reality which has the power of eliciting a life
and death loyalty, i.e., both are not only true but real
religions.

Rosenzweig's position on the messianic status of
Jesus is not without parallel in contemporary Christian
theology. The Catholic theologian, Rosemary Ruether,
writes: "The messianic meaning of Jesus' life, then, is
paradigmatic and proleptic in nature, not final and
fulfilled. It does not invalidate the right of those Jews
not caught up in this paradigm to go forward on earlier
foundations."[32] Like Rosenzweig's paradigm, this shifts
the grounds of disagreement from the simple
declaration that the messiah has or has not come. The
Jewish paradigm focuses on the reality of God and is
willing to wait until the end of history to find out who
the messiah will be--even if it proves to be Jesus
returning. The Christian paradigm, on the other hand,
pays primary attention to Jesus and sees his historical
existence as an anticipation (thus "proleptic") of the
messianic reality and lives in the hope that Jesus will
indeed be gloriously manifested as messiah at the end
of history.

It violates Aristotle's logic to assert two
contradictory positions at the same time and in the
same respect. Thus the statements that the messiah
has come and that the messiah has not come cannot
both be true. This has been and continues to be the

starting point of much Jewish-Christian communication. What is presented here in the Rosenzweig/Ruether model allows for the possibility of both covenantal communities being right. The Christian must remember that the messiah has not come in any final and definitive sense of biblical expectation; but the Christian community lives from the faith and hope that Jesus is the anticipation of the messianic reality and will be its culmination. The Jew hopes only in God and his kingdom and thus has neither interest in nor energy for the issue of an interim kingdom.

All of this leads inevitably to the discussion of mission, specifically the Christian missionizing of Jews. While appropriate in terms of the first model in which either Jews or Christians are wrong, proselytizing seems clearly inappropriate in a context where both can be right, where there can indeed be more than one true religion. This appears as an important concern in Rosenzweig's correspondence with Ehrenberg.

The Mission to the Jews

We begin our investigation here with a long letter written to Hans on June 13, 1918:

> . . . But now to the issue at hand. This time I really do not know where to begin. You see quite rightly, of course, that my far-reaching interest in Christianity is an exception. My *interest, not* my tolerance. (And by tolerance I mean "theological" as well as "ethical" tolerance. How else can religions be tolerant or intolerant but theologically? Christianity, as a missionizing religion, is intolerant regarding religion. Judaism, as a result of its national mysticism rejects the missionizing, which you want to call Judaism's dogmatic heart, and is thereby religiously tolerant and promises 'eternal blessedness to the pious of all the nations.') So, not tolerance but

interest. It is really personal. Christianity
usually has no awareness how little there is of
such interest and are quite bewildered when
some one honestly responds to their question
about what Judaism really thinks about Jesus
with the answer, "nothing at all." As a Jew,
or perhaps I should rather say "as a
theologian" so that I do not make you nervous
again with the opposition of theory and
religion--so, as a theologian, I do not have any
interest at all in Christianity. The case is
quite different insofar as I am an apologist.
That, of course, is a good piece of pure
self-construction. In reality (biographical
reality) I am interested in Christianity because
I was born in Germany, because I've studied
history, because I live in a time in which the
bus boys in the big city and university town
cafes have learned more theology just from
what they pick up than a student of theology
learned from his professors in the 1870's.
Finally, of course, I'm interested in
Christianity because I'm the friend of Rudi etc.
That is biography. And yet this interest does
not remain hermetically sealed in my head;
but because I am a Jew it must lead to
something, whether that be the destruction of
my Jewish existence or its strengthening.
Because the second possibility is what
happened, it becomes apologetics. As a result,
I don't have it in for apologetics as much as
most people--after all, there can also be good
apologetics, why not? Especially in Judaism
one finds that all philosophy of religion has a
certain tendency toward apologetics, since
Judaism (unlike Christianity) is fundamentally
not expansive and therefore is restricted to the
defensive. Most of our summa's are summa's
"against the Gentiles."[33] You seem surprised
at the fact that this apologetics apparently

leads to a standpoint between the religions. But that is only a consequence of striving to do apologetics in good scholarly fashion. Paganism, for example, really gives me a lot more headaches than Christianity. These days when I find passages in Hesiod's *Works and Days*, I work more on them than on the entire New Testament taken together. So as an apologist, I come in practice to the same body of material as a Christian systematic theologian. But I ask questions quite differently. I draw borders and always again borders. I do not reproduce; I only copy. In this process of drawing borders, Christianity naturally comes into the innermost circle. It is only the innermost circle which first separates it from Judaism. Of course, that cannot be any other way. For I think "in scholarly fashion" as a European (or German) from 1900 and therefore I do not compare rationalistically free. Rather, from the first, I fight through history the objects of comparison right up to their prescribed order. This apologetical thinking rules me now so strongly that it is quite possible that my whole theology flows as well into this form. But I do not know that and, in general, not one line or letter is on paper of this whole apologetic. And I do not know in the least which literary form this will take. It is possible that it will be totally theological. Before I am absolutely sure about this, I do not write a single letter. And besides, there is a war going on. At any rate, my birth of tolerance is certainly not un-Jewish, whereas the mentality out of which the current 'science of comparative religions' works is un-Christian. I'm referring here to something like Troeltsche's maxim of Christianity as the religion of western civilization. The Jewish principle of tolerance allows such a journey of discovery through humanity, as the Christian missionary principle demands it. You can see that the Christian system is truly dependent on the command to missionize from the fact that it has a limit where its tolerant understanding stops completely. The Christian scholar of religion can feel empathetic towards just about everything--totem, fetish, taboo, psyche, tao, nirvana. But he can never feel empathetic towards what lies closest to Christianity, namely Judaism. All that he can hold on to is a detail taken out of context. But it is the context which is absolutely incomprehensible for him. Why? Because even here it is not the missionary's right to understand. This mission to the Jews does not grasp the Jews as Jews, but as de-judaised, when it is honest enough to admit this. And it is not the mission to the Jews of the missionaries to the Jews but the only successful mission, the mission of the state, of the society, of the culture. The so-called mission to the Jews, which seeks to latch on to Judaism, can at best catch the ignorant. On the other hand, the mission to the pagans which is conducted with the same methods finds success with the 'best' pagans. There is a way from Platonism to Christianity, but not from rabbinics.

With the contrast of esoteric-exoteric one blurs the reality Judaism-Christianity. It is only from the perspective of today that Judaism is esoteric; the future wants it just as esoteric as Christianity. But now it lays all the stress on the future and therefore feels itself to be exoteric (and therefore is--this 'therefore' is a great realization--also mainly rationalistic) and can bring its esotericism to consciousness only in thought. As a Christian, you concentrate your feeling more or less on today, carry that over automatically to Judaism and ask: What are you doing with the consciousness of your esotericism only in feelings? The answer again: 'absolutely nothing.' You may be completely right: without Christianity, Judaism would not be there. (We will know that quite certainly only when the messiah will come.) But should it be so important for the Jew always to have only a knowledge-bound view so that he would have to come to an understanding with his "believing consciousness?" Your presumption of considering the world and the view of the world so extremely important is again Christian, not Jewish. The Christian celebrates the first day of creation every week--so significant is for him this world still standing there in its toddler shoes--and he reproaches the Jew with denying the idea of creation, simply because the Jew celebrates the seventh day, creation's day of fulfillment. The celebrating of Sunday should infuse every workday with the consciousness and the courage of the beginning--that is the essence of Christianity. The Sabbath should teach every workday to persevere to the end and to be certain that it will come. But when I'm certain of the fulfillment 'with perfect certainty' why should the way to it be so terribly interesting to me? There's no comparison between the finite and the infinite. The certainty of the end is without limit; the interest in the way (even when in my opinion it's very great) is limited. It's only from the viewpoint of Sunday that your description of Judaism as being without faith in creation is understandable. From the viewpoint of the Sabbath, the Christian appears as a human being who really understands nothing about the creation, for he does not understand it in the form 'the heaven and the earth were finished, and all their array.' Genesis 2:1 And only the fulfilled creation is the real one. And, therefore, from the Jewish perspective in which the coming of the messiah is not the end but the fulfillment of the world, the 'days of the messiah' are sharply distinguished from the 'world to come' of eternal happiness.[34]

It seems to be a premise of Rosenzweig in this letter that the Christian mission to the Jews has been a defining element of Christian consciousness, one which it will not be easy for Christianity to relinquish, even in the "Johannine age." Why have Christians become more tolerant towards totem and fetish than towards Jew and Judaism? Possibly because Christians approach the former without presuppositions but they inevitably understand the latter from their own perspective. As Rosenzweig points out, Christians can never understand Jews as Jews.

Why does this happen with Judaism but not with Taoism or an African tribal religion? Because the Christian story includes judgments about the Jews and Judaism but none regarding African tribal religions or Taoism. Jews and Judaism are not neutral objects of reflection for Christians. They are understood essentially as the people who made the wrong judgment about their fellow Jew, Jesus. They are the people who rejected their own messiah, denied the light, read their own scripture with eyes veiled to its deepest meaning. Christianity has no way of talking about Jews and Judaism except as the people who have misunderstood God's deepest salvational plan.

Misunderstanding is actually the most euphemistic description of their choice. It is a stubbornness, a blindness, something ultimately explicable only through a diabolical alliance, finally describable only as the most heinous of crimes, deicide, the killing of God. What then can rescue Christianity from this inescapably baneful posture towards Jews and Judaism? How can Christianity's "good news" cease being a "bad news" for Jews? Certainly through the theology of dual covenant implicit in Rosenzweig's revelational theology. Certainly through the position defined by Rosenzweig in this correspondence whereby both religions can be true, even though only one is real for its adherents.

It is imperative to develop the radical implication of this thesis. It means that in the life-world of Jesus both the people rejecting him and the people following him could have been faithful to God's salvational plan and providence. Neither Christian nor Jew are accustomed to thinking this way. The pharisees walking away from Jesus and the disciples walking with him are both on God-ordained paths, paths that lead on the one hand to Jabneh and its yeshiva and on the other to Syrian Antioch and the first community called "Christian."

The divergent paths remain true along their respective trajectories. As Rosenzweig indicates in this letter, the Christian Sunday has something true to communicate, no less than the Jewish Sabbath. "Today" can truly be stressed in one community, even as the "end of days" is truly proclaimed in the other. The recognition of this in the dawning "Johannine age" would entail simultaneously the rationale for a definitive abandonment by Christians of the mission to the Jews and a new birth of Jewish-Christian understanding.

This is by no means all of the correspondence which Rosenzweig exchanged with Ehrenberg. And, of course, half of the correspondence is not even available; namely, Ehrenberg's letters to Rosenzweig. Nevertheless, what has been translated here can help us gain some sense of the "journey of discovery" on which these two men so courageously embarked and its abiding relevance for Jewish-Christian dialogue.

Not theories about dialogue but the process itself is what Rosenzweig considered primary. This is why the actual exchange of letters seems fitting to a discussion of Rosenzweig's thought and its implications for Jewish-Christian dialogue. Here we see Rosenzweig as a *Sprachdenker*, one who thinks in the context of speaking, one who responds to the demands of the particular historical moment with all its challenges and possibilities. One may disagree with one or other of Rosenzweig's theories but it is difficult to oppose the brilliance and tenacity, the openness and sensitivity, which this modern man of faith brings to this interfaith project.

CHAPTER FOUR

Notes

1. See Rosenstock-Huessy, *Judaism Despite Christianity*.

2. Some of the Rosenzweig/Hans Ehrenberg correspondence has been translated in Glatzer, *Franz Rosenzweig: His Life and Thought*. I have restricted myself in this chapter to material not found there. Some of this material is translated by Walter Jacob in his chapter on Rosenzweig in *Christianity through Jewish Eyes* (Cincinnati: Hebrew Union College Press, 1974).

3. It is tempting to include Rosenzweig's correspondence with his other cousin, Rudolf Ehrenberg, in this chapter, since Rosenzweig often refers to the letters between himself and the two Ehrenbergs as a triangular correspondence. But limitations of space suggest the restriction here to Franz's letters to Hans.

4. Rosenzweig, *Briefe und Tagebücher*, I-1, p. 556. Translation my own.

5. The date in the *Namenverzeichnis* in Rosenzweig, *Briefe und Tagebücher*, I-2, p. 1269 places Hans' birth in 1893, instead of 1883. This is clearly wrong and inconsistent with Rosenzweig's paternal family tree at the end of the same volume.

6. Read, for example, the letter of November 11, 1909 which is found in Glatzer, *Franz Rosenzweig: His Life and Thought*, p. 19.

7. Rosenzweig, *Briefe und Tagebücher*, I-1, pp. 547-548. Translation my own.

8. One notices the intended irony here. Christianity understands itself as quintessentially a religion of brotherly love and its inclination in a generous mood would be to admit or suggest that Judaism *too* teaches love of neighbor.

9. The "it", of course, is the subject of religion.

10. *Nebbish* is an untranslatable Yiddish word most commonly used for a person of no consequence.

11. This single sentence from this letter is also found translated in Glatzer, *Franz Rosenzweig: His Life and Thought*, p. 64.

12. Rosenzweig, *Briefe und Tagebücher*, I-1, pp. 500-501. Translation my own.

13. cf., for example, Arthur Cohen, *The Myth of the Judeo-Christian Tradition* (New York: Harper & Row, 1957).

14. Rosenzweig uses the word *Germanenchristentum*. The *Germanen*, of course, are not the contemporary Germans but the ancient Germans whom we generally refer to in English as Teutons.

15. A reference to World War I, six months from its end, with its constant changing of territorial borders.

16. Rosenzweig, *Briefe und Tagebücher*, I-1, pp. 554-556. Translation my own.

17. Rosenstock-Huessy, *Judaism Despite Christianity*, p. 21.

18. Rosenstock-Huessy, *Judaism Despite Christianity*, p. 158.

19. Rosenzweig, *Briefe und Tagebücher*, I-1, p. 146. Translation my own.

20. Rosenzweig, *Briefe und Tagebücher*, I-1, p. 146.

21. *The Star of Redemption*, p. 412. The reference in Paul is: 1 Corinthians 15:28, "When all things are subjected to him, then the Son himself will also be subjected to him who put all things under him, that God may be everything to everyone." The Greek *panta en pasi* is capable of both translations: "Everything to everyone" or "all-in-all." Translations of the Christian Testament used in this work are from the Revised Standard Version.

22. These two essays by Tertullian are called in English: "Concerning the Soul" and "Concerning the Resurrection of the Body."

23. Rosenzweig, *Briefe und Tagebücher*, I-1, pp. 558-560. Translation my own.

24. The truth in this prophecy is evident in developments both within Catholic and Protestant spirituality. One calls to mind, for example, the works of Pierre Teilhard de Chardin and Jurgen Moltmann. Or one can see this same theme developed in Robert McAfee Brown's excellent *Spirituality and Liberation* (Philadelphia: Westminster Press, 1988).

25. The quotation is from the daily prayer in the Synagogue.

26. Rosenzweig, *Briefe und Tagebücher*, I-1, pp. 560-562. Translation my own.

27. We do not know the exact meaning of Rosenzweig's reference to reading about this un-person in the newspaper but perhaps this refers to instances in

which Jews were blamed for Germany's failure to achieve an early victory in the war. This, of course, is the precise trajectory of European consciousness which was to be developed by the Nazis for whom the Jew is quite literally both *Untermensch* (sub-human) and ultimately *Unmensch* (nonhuman).

28. *The Star*, p. 20.

29. Rosenzweig writes this in Latin: "Extra Ecclesiam nulla salus nisi Judaeis in religione eorum manentibus." He thereby uses the words of the ancient (and controversial) statement of the dogma, adding the exception clause basic to his position from the time of his decision to remain a Jew.

30. Rosenzweig writes the word in Greek. It is the New Testament term used by Paul for those Christians who, in his judgment, impose too many legal observances on Gentile converts.

31. Rosenzweig, *Briefe und Tagebücher*, I-1, pp. 543-44. Translation my own.

32. Rosemary Radford Ruether, *Faith and Fratricide* (New York: Seabury Press, 1974), p. 249.

33. Rosenzweig uses the Latin, referring thereby to Thomas Aquinas' *Summa Contra Gentiles* which was really a handbook for missionaries working with Moslems. Aquinas, of course, uses *gentiles* to refer to non-Christians, reflecting the ancient Christian view that Christianity constitutes the new Israel.

34. Rosenzweig, *Briefe und Tagebücher*, I-1, pp. 577-580.

CHAPTER FIVE

STEPS TOWARDS DIALOGUE

Born near the end of the nineteenth century and maturing during the early years of the twentieth, Franz Rosenzweig achieved a level of Jewish-Christian dialogue that it will be the challenge of the twenty-first century to surpass. Meanwhile, it remains to us, in the few remaining years of this century, to assimilate the full implications of Rosenzweig's position and to emulate the boldness of his vision.

A major step in that direction was taken by Paul van Buren in his multi-volume work entitled *A Theology of the Jewish-Christian Reality*.[1] This eminent Protestant theologian challenges us with the realization that in all of its 2000 years, Christianity has never produced a theology of the people Israel. At first blush, this seems absurd, since there have been countless Christian theologies of Judaism, beginning with Paul's Letter to the Romans and continuing through the "Contra Judaeos" tractates of the patristic period to later interpretations. But van Buren's point, of course, is that these have not been theologies born of dialogue, of listening to the other faith community's witness to God, and of accepting that testimony as valid theological evidence in its own right.

What van Buren means by a Christian theology of Israel must be an integral part of the church's self-critical reality and ask "about the church's duty and ability to hear the testimony of the Jewish people to God."[2] This means, of course, really listening to the

121

Jewish people with respect and openness, even when they are expressing a resounding "no" to the Christian message and claim. Van Buren makes it clear that Christians are not to presume to define Judaism for Jews (another characteristic of most of the prior Christian "theologies of Judaism") but, after listening to Judaism's testimony, to address the topic of the people of Israel within their own Christian faith community, as something Christians need to talk about among themselves.[3]   From the Jewish perspective, Rabbi Marc Tanenbaum underscores this need for Christian theologians to "develop a theology of Israel and the synagogue in salvation history that has some correspondence with the historic realities of the present-day living Jewish people."[4]

Christianity has said a great deal about Judaism in its two thousand-year history. But in these instances, Judaism has inevitably been defined in terms of Christianity's own identity and faith. Just as women in our western tradition from Aristotle through Aquinas were defined as biologically deficient males, Jews were understood by Christians as the people who did not recognize their own Messiah when he came. They were the unfaithful people, in contrast to the faithful Christians.   Judaism was constantly Christianity's foil, the scapegoat for Christianity's failures in faith, the projection of Christianity's shadow.[5]   Christianity was a religion of the spirit and Judaism one of the flesh. Christians knew they were saved by faith but Jews attempted to save themselves through their works. Christians carried the "easy yoke" of the gospel, while Jews labored under the burdensome yoke of the law. Christianity's good news, in other words, was always simultaneously a "bad news" for the Jews.[6]

Judaism was not much different in its reactions to Christianity.   Until the time of Franz Rosenzweig, Judaism's most generous evaluation of Christianity was achieved through its use of the Noahide covenant formulation. The source of this is the covenant God made with Noah, as that story is told in the ninth chapter of

Genesis; it is generally interpreted by the rabbis to include seven basic precepts: prohibitions against idolatry, blasphemy, killing, stealing, sexual sins, eating the limb of a living animal, and the positive commandment to set up courts of justice.[7] This theology, though generous toward Christians in one respect, does not deal with Christianity in its uniqueness, seeing it rather as simply another form of Gentile existence. Yes, Gentiles can be saved and even be righteous by their fulfillment of the covenant given through Noah to all human beings. And Christians, as a subset of the category Gentile, have that same possibility. And yet that is hardly a theology of Christianity, i.e., a theology born from listening to how Christians talk about themselves, nor does it approach the stature of Rosenzweig's recognition of the validity of God's covenantal action through Jesus and the consequent status of Christianity as a true religion.

"What is true in Christianity is not new, and what is new is not true."[8] With few exceptions, this was the characteristic Jewish attitude toward Christianity. Maimonides can quote Talmudic authority in arguing that "...every man who ennobles his soul with excellent morals and wisdom based on the faith in God, certainly belongs to the men of the world to come."[9] The Talmudic text he is alluding to there is Bava Kamma 38a: "Even a non-Jew who studies the Torah of our teacher Moses resembles a High Priest." This recognition of a Christian as a non-Jew is not, of course, the same as what is sought for in true dialogue. And Rabbi Jacob Emden (1697-1776), commenting on a Talmudic statement to the effect that every assembly that is for the sake of heaven will last, wrote of Christianity and Islam: "Their assembly is also for the sake of Heaven, to make Godliness known amongst the nations, to speak of Him in distant places. . . ."[10] Generous words from exceptional rabbis, but nonetheless inadequate in appreciating Christianity's own self-definition.

ECCLESIASTICAL STATEMENTS

It is Jewish thinkers who have the ultimate responsibility of listening to Christians and developing their
own theologies about Christianity from the vantage
point of Jewish faith, just as it is their task to articulate their own religious existence in the world as
Jews.[11]   It falls to the lot of Christian theologians, on
the other hand, not only to give an account of Christian
faith, but to address the continuing witness of their
elder brothers and sisters to a covenanting God.   Van
Buren is by no means alone among Christian theologians in attempting to do precisely this.   Some of the
outstanding people doing this work today with whom I
have spoken include Gregory Baum, Clemens Thoma,
Rosemary Ruether, and John Pawlikowski.   The work
of these individual theologians, of course, tends to be
significantly   in   advance   of   official   ecclesiastical
statements.[12]

History may have been made in this regard by
something first reported in *The New York Times*: the
announcement that the United Church of Christ had
become the first major Protestant denomination in the
United States to reject Christianity's traditional replacement theology.   The declaration adopted on Tues-
day, June 30, 1987 at a meeting in Cleveland, Ohio
included the recognition that the Christian Church has
frequently "denied God's continuing covenantal relationship with the Jewish people expressed in the faith
of Judaism."   After asking for God's forgiveness, the
document then states explicitly that "Judaism has not
been superseded by Christianity" and Christianity is
not to be understood "as the successor religion to
Judaism."[13]

Is this simply the first statement of this kind by "a
major Protestant denomination in the United States" or
is it indeed a milestone for any Christian ecclesiastical
group, including the largest Christian denomination, the
Roman Catholic Church?   Since the Roman Catholic
tradition is my own, I felt a special urgency to re-

examine the 1964 text of the Second Vatican Council, the official Guidelines and Suggestions for Implementing the Conciliar Declaration "Nostra Aetate" that appeared in 1974, and more recent statements by the present Bishop of Rome, John Paul II. Do any of these texts include a confession of Christian sins against the Jews? Do any of these documents affirm God's continuing covenantal relationship with the Jewish people in such a way as to deny that Judaism has been superseded by Christianity, thereby repudiating the traditional replacement theology or supersessionism of Christian thought? Finally, do any of these statements mitigate the teaching that human salvation is found exclusively in Jesus?

Nostra Aetate

The "Declaration on the Relationship of the Church to Non-Christian Religions" carries a history of palace intrigue from its inception in Pope John XXIII's desire to have the Council make a statement on the Jews, to some tense moments when it looked as though there would be no statement at all, to the final compromise document which was officially voted on by some two thousand bishops and promulgated by Pope Paul VI on October 28, 1965. In the recently published journals kept by Thomas Merton during these historic years of 1964 and 1965, the renowned Trappist comments in his journal entry for September 10, 1964:

Abraham Heschel has sent me a memo on the new Jewish Chapter at the Vatican Council. The new proposal is incredibly bad. All the meaning has been taken out of it. All the originality, all the light are gone and it has become a stuffy, pointless piece of formalism with the stupid addition that the Church is looking forward with hope to the union of Jews with herself. . . . This lack of spiritual and eschatological sense, this unawareness of the real need for profound change, is what makes such statements pitiable. One feels a total lack of prophetic insight and even of elementary compunction. Where is the prophetic and therefore deeply humiliated and humanly impoverished thirst for light, that Christians and Jews may begin to find some kind of unity in seeking God's will together? But if Rome simply declares herself complacently to be the mouthpiece of God and perfect interpreter of God's will for the Jews, with the implication that He in no way ever speaks to them directly, this is simply monstrous![14]

Though he met an untimely death in 1968, Merton continues to play a prophetic role in this area of Church life as in so many others. Not only does this statement far outshine anything in *Nostra Aetate* but it continues to shed more light on Jewish-Christian relations than anything I have seen in subsequent Vatican documents and papal statements on Jews and Judaism to date.[15]

The justly criticized and politically tarnished *Nostra Aetate* follows the most benign side of the Christian tradition since the writings of the apostle Paul in praising Judaism for what it was *before Christ*. The Jews, as Paul first expressed it in Romans 11:28 are "beloved for the sake of their forefathers." This has always been easy for Christians to say, since, except for the Marcionites of every generation, the "Old Testament" remains part of the Christian Bible. But the same hermeneutical perspective that calls the Tanakh the "Old Testament" assimilates the Hebraic story for Christian purposes.[16]

The conciliar document states, for example, that "the salvation of the Church was mystically foreshadowed by the chosen people's exodus from the land of bondage."[17] This approach is doubly disadvantageous to Judaism. First, this paradigm event of Jewish history is perceived through a Christian lens and not acknowledged on its own terms. Whatever the Exodus means to Jews, it does not mean the "salvation of the Church." Secondly, this constant praising of Judaism before Christ leads to a Christian amnesia about the last two thousand years of Jewish existence. There is no praise for the writers of the Talmud in the first few centuries of the Common Era, for the Jewish martyrs who died sanctifying God's name during the Crusades or in countless Christian persecutions and pogroms, for the Jewish mystics who profoundly lived the way of Torah in every century from the time of Christ to our own. And it is this amnesia that produced the myth of "late Judaism," the term long used by Christian scholars to describe Judaism at the time of Jesus. It was, of course, "late" only from a perspective in which Judaism ended with the mission and message of Jesus.

The Council document reaffirms the Christian position that the Jews failed to recognize their Messiah when he came. "Jerusalem did not recognize the time of her visitation."[18] There is no doubt but that the Council's perspective recognizes only one valid and true faith community. The same sentence clearly indicates that Christianity is indeed the successor religion to Judaism by stating that "the Church is the new people of God."[19] Anti-Semitism is rejected but without the repentance of the United Church of Christ's statement. Rabbi Marc Tanenbaum makes this point very eloquently: "Overriding all, however, was the absence in the Declaration of any note of contrition or repentance for the incredible sufferings and persecutions Jews have undergone in the Christian West."[20]

There is a strange sense of disassociation in the text, for anti-Jewish persecution is condemned "at any time and from any source"[21] but without the obvious recognition that a crucial "time" was the two thousand years in which a large part of the Jewish community lived in "Christian" Europe and a major "source" was the very same ecclesiastical group now sitting in solemn session to ratify the document. It is a sad and disturbing fact that 245 of the assembled bishops voted against the statement adopted by the majority that "Jews should not be presented as repudiated or cursed by God."[22] So what was being condemned "at any time and from any source" was actually taking place at that very moment and within that very assembly.

There is no movement in this text away from the concept of the exclusivity of salvation through Christ. "Christ in His boundless love freely underwent His passion and death because of the sins of all men, so that all might attain salvation."[23] In short, there is nothing here remotely close to what is contained in the statement of the United Church of Christ, neither a prayer for God's forgiveness for the anti-Jewishness of the Church's own history, nor any real affirmation of the ongoing validity of God's covenant with the Jews, nor any suggestion that Judaism has not been superseded by Christianity and somehow absorbed within its salvational scheme.

Some would counter the apparent harshness of this judgment by urging that the text clearly states, echoing Romans 11:28-29, that "the Jews still remain most dear to God, because of their fathers, for He does not repent of the gifts He makes nor of the calls He issues."[24] I wish I could agree with those theologians who see this as an affirmation of the ongoing validity of Israel's covenant with God. In my reading, however, that is neither the intention of Paul nor the obvious implication of the text. Since the beginning of the verse where the Jews are called "enemies of God" is omitted, I would argue that the meaning here is indeed that God continues to love the Jews and does not abandon his covenantal commitment to them, for, in one or another mysterious way, they will eventually be brought into the covenant sealed in the blood of Jesus. Neither the Jews' being loved by God nor God's continuing faithfulness to his gifts and calls implies the ongoing validity of the Sinai covenant as constituting Judaism *post Christum* as a true religion and a legitimate, independent path of salvation. Jews continue to be loved, but precisely for the role they will play in the Christian scenario of salvation history.

CONCILIAR GUIDELINES OF 1974

On December 1, 1974, the Commission for Religious Relations with the Jews, under the leadership of Cardinal Willebrands, published "Guidelines and Suggestions for Implementing the Conciliar Declaration *Nostra Aetate*."[25]   The first page of this document takes a positive step toward dialogue by suggesting that Christians educate themselves to Jewish self-definition: "They [Christians] must strive to learn by what essential traits the Jews define themselves in the light of their own religious experience."[26]   Christian mission to the Jews is not repudiated but is to be conducted "while maintaining the strictest regard for religious liberty. . ."[27]   This opened the door for the distinction between proselytism and witness expressed by Tommaso Federici, when he addressed an international meeting of Catholic-Jewish dialogue in Venice two years after this statement was issued.[28]

Although the document lacks a real confession of guilt, tentative steps in that direction are taken by mention of "an unfortunate past" and encouragement to Christians "to see to what extent the responsibility is theirs. . ."[29]   And the text boldly suggests an area of parity between the two religions by stating: "The idea of a living community in the service of God, and in the service of men for the love of God, such as it is realized in the liturgy is just as characteristic of the Jewish liturgy as it is of the Christian one."[30]   Statements like this, indicating parallels between Christianity and other religions, are both rare and deeply significant for an emerging dialogue.

Unlike the conciliar statement, this document acknowledges Judaism *post Christum*, although in a very guarded way. Not prepared yet to say that Judaism is still a valid covenantal community, much less an authentic path of salvation, this 1974 text nonetheless states that: "The history of Judaism did not end with the destruction of Jerusalem, but rather went on to develop a religious tradition."[31] Although this statement carefully chooses the phrase "religious tradition," rather than "religion," much less "a true religion," even this minimal admission is a significant recovery of the two thousand-year memory lapse so characteristic of Christian consciousness about Jews and Judaism.

In terms of the three most significant points in the United Church of Christ statement--the confession of sin, the acknowledgment of Judaism as a valid covenantal community, and the repudiation of replacement theology--the Guidelines clearly fall short of anything comparable. Nevertheless, subtle indications of the sort we have examined suggest a greater openness to the consideration of issues like these. It is, after all, asking a great deal of a commission to initiate a theological change of such magnitude as the rejection of the Church's two thousand-year self-understanding as Judaism's religious successor.

Recent Catholic Statements

It was on November 17, 1980 that Pope John Paul II addressed German Catholics in Mainz. He took as a theme of his address a statement from a declaration by the German bishops: "Who meets Jesus Christ, meets Judaism."[32] It is extremely important to note here the departure from traditional language; it is not the "Old Testament" nor the Hebrew legacy but Judaism that one encounters in meeting Jesus Christ. Although this is significant, even in 1980, we cannot help but reflect on what an extraordinary difference this could have made in an official statement by the German bishops or by the Pope fifty years earlier.

The Pope goes on to speak of Jesus as "the son of David and son of Abraham."[33] He explicitly acknowledges Franz Rosenzweig and Martin Buber "who through their creative familiarity with the Hebrew and with the German languages established a truly admirable bridge for a profound encounter between the two cultures."[34] Again, this is a significantly new step, naming Jewish scholars (German Jews, since the address is in Mainz), who indeed paved the way for the level of Jewish-Christian dialogue possible today. This posthumous compliment to Franz Rosenzweig encourages Jews and Christians alike.

The Pope refers to the Jews as "the people of God of the old covenant never retracted by God."[35] The scriptural reference supporting this is again Romans 11:29: "For the gifts and the call of God are irrevocable." This text, as we have seen, is a *locus classicus* for any Christian seeking canonical support for positive statements about Jews. Being loved by God, however, does not preclude the possibility that God's love calls them to conversion. Nevertheless, Pope John Paul II uses the text here to make a different point, placing more emphasis on the ongoing validity of the Sinai covenant (even though it is still called "the old covenant") and at least suggesting a continuing independent validity for Jewish religious existence.

He later refers to the Jews as "today's people of the covenant concluded with Moses."[36] This seems to imply that Jews today live their religious existence through the covenant mediated by Moses. Here it is not even called an "old" covenant nor is there any suggestion of its being replaced. Roman documents are known for their ability to introduce changes in subtle and oblique ways, so that the impression is given at one level that nothing is different. And yet, this kind of phrase, employed in an official address by the chief pastor of the Roman Church, indicates a movement in Catholic thought toward the recognition of Judaism *post Christum*. It is all the more remarkable, and yet consistent with Vatican policy, that no trumpet is blown to suggest this dramatic shift.

Two years after this Mainz address, the Pope spoke in Rome on the topic of "The Importance of Jewish-Christian Relations." This was an ecumenical gathering, including representatives of the Orthodox Churches, the Anglican Communion, the Lutheran World Federation, and the World Council of Churches. After recounting some of the positive statements in Paul's Letter to the Romans, John Paul II says that: ". . . the links between the church and the Jewish people are grounded in the design of the God of the covenant."[37] Again, the admission is not explicit, but the suggestion is there that the continuing existence of the Jewish community is more than the opportunity to repent of their failure to recognize their Messiah when he came. Perhaps the stubborn refusal of Israel to believe in Jesus as messiah is more than a mysterious plan of God to allow more Gentiles to enter the community of salvation and eventually prompt the remaining Jews, through jealousy of what God is doing among the Gentiles, to seek conversion. It is possible that the existence of the two communities, separate but linked in countless ways, is indeed the design of God.

In the next paragraph of the text, the Pope falls short of making the straight-forward confession of sin risked by the United Church of Christ. The language seems frustratingly evasive. "*If* there have been misunderstandings, errors, and even insults since the day of separation. . ."[38] Why this ever-present *if*? Without indicating that any of the persecutors were Christians, the Bishop of Rome goes on to say: "The terrible persecutions suffered by the Jews in various periods of history have finally opened many eyes and disturbed many hearts."[39] Why is the word *Christian* so glaringly absent in this sentence? Were any of those terrible persecutions perpetrated by Christians? Were any Christian eyes opened or Christian hearts disturbed? Though falling short of that honest admission of sin still so disturbingly absent in official Catholic documents, these statements are encouraging in their willingness to begin to look at Jewish reality with open eyes.

The Pope disassociates his conciliatory gestures from what he refers to as "a certain religious relativism."[40] He reaffirms the exclusive salvational claim of Christianity: "Christians profess their faith without equivocation in the universal salvific character of the death and resurrection of Jesus of Nazareth."[41] This is certainly compatible with a kind of dialogue, not the kind developed by Franz Rosenzweig or hoped for by many of today's theologians, both Jewish and Christian, but certainly something better than what preceded it. The Pope concludes by saying: "We shall be able to go by diverse--but in the end, convergent--paths with the help of the Lord, who has never ceased loving his people to reach true brotherhood in reconciliation, respect, and full accomplishment of God's plan in history."[42]

The final document we will consider in this brief overview of Catholic pronouncements is colloquially referred to as *Notes*; its official title is: *Commission for Religious Relations with the Jews: Notes on the Correct Way to Present the Jews and Judaism in Preaching and Catechesis in the Roman Catholic Church, 1985.*[43] The text reflects the current ambivalence in the Church often seen as embodied in John Cardinal Willebrands and Joseph Cardinal Ratzinger. Willebrands, President of the Secretariat for Christian Unity, has been active in Jewish-Christian dialogue since the stormy debates of the Vatican Council. He represents the liberal side of the Catholic tradition, an influence that has been waning in recent years.[44] Ratzinger, of course, has become symbolic of the reactionary and repressive tendencies within the Church through his inquisitional attacks on theologians of the caliber of Charles Curran, Leonardo Boff, and Matthew Fox. The tension of a Church caught between these two influences is reflected in current Vatican pronouncements, including *Notes*.

Charting these two diverse currents of theological opinion provides the best summary of *Notes*. In line with the Willebrands' tradition, we find several encouraging sentiments. Catholics are challenged to "*pastoral* concern for a still living reality closely related to the Church."[45] Any reading of the scriptures that juxtaposes "Old" and "New" Testament passages polemically is rejected and we are reminded that: "The Church, in the spontaneity of the Spirit which animates her, has vigorously condemned the attitude of Marcion and always opposed his dualism."[46] Rosenzweig would certainly have approved the statement that "the people of the Old and the New Testament are tending toward a like end in the future: the coming or return of the Messiah--even if they start from two different points of view."[47] Finally, in a tradition that has consistently robbed Jesus of his Judaism, it is encouraging to hear that "Jesus was and always remained a Jew. . . ."[48]

The reactionary tendencies represented by Ratzinger are no less evident in the document. Rosenzweig's dual covenant theology is explicitly rejected: "Church and Judaism cannot then be seen as two parallel ways of salvation and the Church must witness to Christ as the Redeemer for all. . . ."[49] Although anti-Semitism is again rejected, Jews are still understood in their relationship to Christian theology and we are urged to appreciate and love the Jews "who have been chosen by God to prepare the coming of Christ and have preserved everything that was progressively revealed and given in the course of their preparation, notwithstanding their difficulty in recognizing in him their Messiah."[50] This identification of the Jews totally in terms of their relationship to the reality of the Church is a very disappointing return to older modes of thought. No less unenlightened is the very lame footnote in which we are told that the Church continues to use the expression *Old Testament* because it is traditional (so too, of course, are pogroms and ghettos) and because it does not mean "out of date" or "outworn."[51]

What is the source of the replacement theology or supersessionism that has held sway in official Christian theological utterances until our own day? What are the roots of the strange ambivalence about Jews and Judaism so evident in Christian consciousness? All of these questions lead us to a reexamination of the man who stands at the gateway of Christian theology, Saul of Tarsus, better known by his Roman name as Paul.

Paul the Polarizer

I have long wrestled with Paul, pondering the insights of scholars from Bornkamm and Schweitzer to Stendahl and Gaston. There are several currents of Pauline interpretation. Some scholars find Paul anti-Jewish and agree with him. A great deal of Christian polemics continue to derive from that starting point. Other scholars conclude that Paul was not opposed to the Jews but only to those who failed to recognize the fulfillment of God's promises concerning the Gentiles.[52] This argument seems appealing to me but ultimately unconvincing. I find myself increasingly drawn to a third current of thought: Paul was anti-Jewish and he was wrong.

Once I am able to say this, I find in myself both a new appreciation for some dimensions of this man and his message and a new concern for the implications of other aspects of his thought. The depth of his mysticism, the centrality of freedom in his religious experience, the tenderness of his concern for "Gentile sinners," and the power of his understanding of love as action that builds the community--all of this impresses me in a new way. And yet, the harshness of the polemical dimensions of his thought and his inability to operate in a dialogical mode strike me with new force. This latter deficiency proves especially relevant to Jewish-Christian dialogue.

Why was dialogue so difficult for Paul? Was it his temperament or a characteristic of his time? When he was a Pharisee, he was intolerant of apostate Jews. When he joined the ranks of the apostates, he became intolerant of the Judaism represented by the Pharisees. He was a polarizer; people fell in place to his right and left as friends or enemies. The writings of the Christian Testament suggest that as a new convert he experienced conflict with those disciples who had known Jesus in his public ministry, as well as with his fellow missionaries to the Gentiles. He challenges Peter openly at Antioch and mysteriously breaks his brotherly bond with Barnabas.[53]

Who was this polemical Paul? Can Christians accept his letters as canonical and yet not be bound to follow him in his partisan thinking? It seems to me that a crucial element of the challenge facing contemporary Jewish-Christian dialogue hinges on the Christian community's ability to criticize Paul. It was Rosenzweig who gave me a new impetus to reexamine the Pauline legacy. Perhaps he can play that role for other Christian theologians. One thing is certain: there is no avoiding Paul, since his language stamps every subsequent Christian exposition of the Church's relationship to Jews and Judaism.

Beloved Enemies

In trying to understand Christianity's classic replacement theology and the strange ambivalence this faith community has harbored toward its parent religion through the centuries, I am struck by the almost epigrammatic character of a frequently quoted verse from Paul's Letter to the Romans: "As regards the gospel, they [the Jews] are enemies of God for your sake; but as regards election, they are beloved for the sake of their forefathers." (Romans 11:28) The juxtaposition of "enemies" and "beloved" in one verse seems symptomatic of Christianity's posture toward Judaism. To understand this verse is to find access to the deepest stratum of Christian consciousness about the Jews, with its essential ambiguity of love and hate, acceptance and rejection, preservation and replacement.

On the one hand, the Jews are beloved (*agapetoi*). This reveals one side of Christian consciousness. They are forever loved by Christians "because of their forefathers" (*dia tous pateras*). Not for themselves, but because of their heritage. And what is that legacy, that gift from the fathers? First of all, it is Jesus of Nazareth, born of the House of David. Then, it is the Hebrew Bible, which was the Bible of Jesus and which becomes the Christian "Old Testament." And finally, it is the Jewish story that connects this "new religion" to a narrative linked with the very creation of the world. Within these stories we find the great figures of the "Old Testament" who now become the spiritual ancestors of Christian men and women baptized with those names: Abraham and David, Sarah and Rebecca, Joshua and Deborah.

On the other hand, the Jews are enemies (*ecthroi*). And this lays bare the other side of Christian consciousness. Jews are enemies of the gospel. Enemies through their unbelief, their stubborn clinging to the Torah, their failure to accept Jesus as their Messiah. Classical Christian theology does not work with the possibility of a variety of belief systems. In this kind of theological context, one cannot counter that the Jews trust the revelation of Sinai and then understand them through what they believe, rather than through what they don't believe. It is only in recent times, and in precisely the kind of dialogical context which Rosenzweig develops, that one can entertain the possibility of trusting the living God in more than one way. In the polemical thought stretching from Paul to the present, Jewish belief can be understood only as unbelief, and Jews are not people who believe in the way of Torah, but "enemies of the gospel" who do not believe in Jesus.

The gospels were written later than Paul's Letter to the Romans and however vividly they portray the separation between Jesus and his fellow Jews, between the followers of Jesus and the disciples of the Torah, they do not describe a consciousness essentially different

from what we see in Paul. This is why Jesus is almost
never called "a Jew" in the Christian Testament. The
word has already begun to take on the connotation of
one who denies Jesus. Even today, many Christians
use circumlocutions to speak of Jewish acquaintances,
calling them "people of the Jewish faith" or even
"Hebrews," because subconsciously they think of the
word "Jew" as an insult, one of those words that polite
people shouldn't use.

This crucial verse of the Letter to the Romans is
but the culmination and capstone of Paul's reflections
on the Jewish people. The entire epistle merits attention, since it is the wellspring of Christianity's self-
understanding vis-a-vis Judaism. Christian writings
from Chrysostom to the most recent ecclesiastical documents cling to the formulations of this text like needles
to a magnet. It is no wonder. For in Paul we find, if
not the founder of Christianity some claim him to be
the man who, more than any other, deserves to be called the first articulate Christian.[54]

Before, contemporary with, and long after Paul,
there were Jewish sectarians who believed Jesus to be
the Messiah. These Jews constituted what contemporary scholarship often refers to as "the Jesus Movement." Such Jews belonged to a messianic sect but
were nonetheless Jews. They still understood the
center of their religious existence in terms of the
revelation of Sinai. They would have considered
neglecting the prescriptions of *halacha*[55] as an
abandonment of the Torah and ultimately of the God
who first revealed it to Moses. They were, therefore,
observant Jews who believed that Jesus was the
Messiah. One does not cease being a religious Jew by
believing that someone is the Messiah. One ceases
being a religious Jew by abandoning Judaism's revelational center, the Torah.[56]

My claim is not that Paul is the first articulate
member of the Jesus Movement. That initial reaction
to the Christ event may remain without a spokesperson
and indeed finds only residual expression in the Chris-

tian Testament. Paul, to whom the greater part of the Christian Testament canon is attributed, speaks for Christianity. By that I mean a religion distinct from the parent religion of Judaism in the most important way that a religion can be distinct, by having a different symbolic center. Since the center of Judaism is the Torah, we are discussing a religion that has a center other than the Torah. Paul is clearly the first Christian to articulate this development in writings that are extant today.

For Paul, the center of his faith, his reason for trusting God, is not what God did in the Exodus/Sinai events but what God did in Jesus. Paul's gospel is the message of the death and resurrection of Jesus. It is no longer Paul who lives but Christ who lives in him. (Galatians 2:20) An observant Jew wraps himself in the *talit* in his daily prayer, symbolizing the encompassing of his whole being in God's Torah whose *mitzvot* (commandments) are counted in the *tzitzit* or fringes of this prayer shawl. Perhaps this is what Paul is remembering in encouraging Christians to "put on the Lord Jesus Christ," (Romans 13:14) for it is the Christ event not the Sinai event in which the Christian is encompassed.

The Letter to the Romans was written around 57 C.E.[57] Nowhere in Paul's other letters or in the entire Christian Testament can we find a fuller exposition of Christianity, i.e., the religion that proclaims Jesus. This is not the religion *of* Jesus, nor is it the religion of the members of the Jesus Movement. It is the religion *about* Jesus that has been known ever since as Christianity. The Jew who claims that someone is the Messiah can still be a Jew--after all, as great a rabbi as Akiba thought that of Bar Kochba. But the Jew who finds a religious center outside the Torah is an apostate.

From a Jewish perspective, Paul ceases to be a Jew. Not because he claims that Jesus is the Messiah; that would be allowable to a Jew. It is because he is claiming that the center of religious existence is no longer in living the Torah given to Moses at Sinai but accepting Jesus and his death and resurrection as the salvific event for the whole world. This is why Jewish scholarship has traditionally been more sympathetic to Jesus than to Paul. Jesus lived and died a Jew; the same cannot be said of Paul.

What led Paul to step beyond his Judaism? There is probably no one answer, but a study of his letters readily suggests Paul's personal, mystical experience of the risen Christ and whatever communicated to Paul within that experience that he had been elected to bring the message of salvation to the Gentiles. Rosenzweig acknowledges the authenticity of these visions in a passage in his diary:

> The visions of Paul etc. are obviously authentic visions. There really aren't any inauthentic ones. But there are different gods. Only God is eternal. The false gods are dead or will die. And they either war against God or--like "Christ"--they are united with him.[58]

So, according to Rosenzweig, the man whom the Christians call "Christ" is aligned with the true God, and Paul's experience of that Christ is both a real vision and a true one, i.e., both a true religious experience and an experience of the true God.

Paul tells us in Galatians 1:16 that God " was pleased to reveal his Son to me, in order that I might preach him among the Gentiles." It is striking in this passage--and completely consistent with what we learn elsewhere in the epistles--that Paul's revelatory experience brings together the manifestation of God's Son and the mandate to preach that same Christ to the Gentiles. Paul is not called to preach the Torah. Paul claims that it is in the proclamation of Christ that Jews and Gentiles find equal access to the Father.

And yet, as Emil Fackenheim points out:

To be sure, the apostle Paul breaks down all
barriers between Jews and Gentiles, men and
women, free men and slaves. He does so, however, through his Christ, and through Him
alone; hence Paul's universalism, far from
overcoming particularism, retains and in a way
radicalizes it.[59]

The Torah, therefore, serves no further salvific purpose
for Jew or Gentile.

This is a radical insight that now severs Paul and
his followers forever from inclusion in the Jewish community. And yet, part of Paul remains Jewish and continues to affirm that the Jew does have some religious
advantage because of the Torah. In the third chapter
of Romans, Paul asks what advantage they have and
answers that the Jews are entrusted with the oracles of
God. But in that same chapter he goes on to say that
Jews have no real advantage, since Jew and Gentile
alike are under the power of sin. In Romans 9:4 he
tells his readers that "They are Israelites, and to them
belong the sonship, the glory, the covenants, the giving
of the law..." The same law, however, is the object of a
long theological excursus in earlier chapters of Romans
where it is identified with sin, slavery, and death. Can
this ambivalence be resolved? Did Paul ever resolve it?
    My answer to both questions is in the negative.
And I say that not to discredit Paul but to recognize
his greatness as a transitional figure. Martin Luther,
many years after his excommunication, still clung to his
tattered monk's habit, hoping for the mother church--
whom he could sometimes call a whore--to assemble a
council and recognize him as a legitimate son. In a
very real sense, Luther never became a Lutheran. Nor
was Paul ever to achieve a Christian identity allowing
him to dismiss Judaism as totally and unequivocally as
his successors did. Men like Luther and Paul were
condemned to live between paradigms, struggling to

give birth to the new, while feeling the pain of letting go of the old.

Martin Luther wanted to be a Catholic Christian, even while he was fathering the German Reformation. Paul of Tarsus wanted to be a Jew, even while he was creating an inseparable gulf between Jews and Christians. This ambivalence remained with Paul to the end and it is reflected in all of his writings. This is precisely the "friends but enemies" mentality alluded to earlier. This ambivalence lives on in most Christians. Part of Christian consciousness is always praising the "Old Testament" and the patriarchs; part of that same consciousness is either condemning Jews to hell or promising them ultimate salvation through conversion. Conversion, of course, means no longer being Jews, i.e., no longer believing that the central expression of their faithfulness to God is the living of the Torah. It is the old conundrum with which Jews have been faced for so many centuries and in so many forms. How can we accept a friendship which demands as its price the dissolution of our identity?

Paul's Synthesis

Paul attempts a synthesis--one that I feel is finally unsuccessful--with faith as the vital bridge between the old and the new. *Emunah* is the ancient Hebrew word for *faith*, indicating a trusting forward of one's life rather than the affirmation of a creedal proposition, *fiducia* rather than *fides*, an existential posture rather than a cerebral formulation. In Romans, as well as Galatians, Paul harkens back to the words of the prophet Habakkuk: "The righteous person shall live by his faith."[60] The verse can also be translated, "The person who through faith is righteous shall live." The latter translation better fits the polemic of the Reformation but is less obvious in the original prophetic oracle.

We should take a moment with the word *righteous*. It is an unfortunate word, living so closely to its neighbor *self-righteous*. We make no progress at all by using the other common translation, *just*, and speaking of the process of *being made just* as *justification*. My own tendency in translation is wherever possible to seek a word found in conversational usage. None of us would refer to a religious person we deeply respect and admire as either a righteous or a just man or woman. But we might use a word like *God-centered*. "Behold, he whose soul is not upright in him shall fail, but the righteous shall live by his faith." (Habakkuk 2:4) God-centered people shall live by their trust in the divine, even when human hopes fail.

Paul correctly understands that this trust is the basis of all God-centeredness. He returns to this theme in the fourth chapter of Romans where he argues that Abraham's God-centeredness was based on his faith as well. Paul read and quoted Genesis 15:6 where we are told that Abraham believed the Lord, and God "reckoned it to him as righteousness." The history of Judaism begins with the patriarch Abraham who trusted the God who called him and covenanted with him. Subsequent generations of Jews continued to recognize God as the God of Abraham, of Isaac, and of Jacob.

Paul would have received no real argument from his Jewish contemporaries on this point. "Trusting in God" clearly describes the fundamental posture of a believing Jew. Paul, however, wants to move that trust in a new direction. His followers are called to trust in that same God because of what he has done in Jesus. At first blush, this might seem to constitute the basis for exactly the kind of dual covenant theology we discussed earlier. Jews trust in the Divine because of what God did in the Exodus/Sinai event and this leads them to a faithful living of the Torah. Christians trust in the Divine because of what God did in the Jesus event and this leads them to live the covenant made in Jesus' blood.

Certain questions cry to be answered at this juncture. What if Paul had presented his good news in such a way that it was not bad news for the Jews who did not choose to convert? What if he had expressed his own experience of identification with the risen Christ without trying to deprecate the Torah-faithful experience of the Jews? Perhaps those who were called to covenant in Jesus' name might have lived at peace with those called to covenant in the Torah given to Moses. Perhaps we could be looking back on two thousand years of fruitful dialogue and mutual enrichment, instead of two thousand years of polemics, persecutions, and pogroms. A theology of dual covenant could have flourished centuries before the birth of Franz Rosenzweig. And his wife and son might not have had to flee the last and most terrible wave of anti-Semitism following in the wake of the exclusivist theology inherited from Paul, Luther, and countless other Christians.

Is Paul then the father of "born-again Christians," the vocal Evangelicals so prominent in the contemporary religious scene?[61] In one sense, yes. At least in so far as Paul expresses an exclusivist view of salvation. There is only one mode of salvation and that is faith in what God has done in Jesus Christ. Jews who don't have that faith cannot be saved (despite all the benefits that they have received) and that is a fortiori true of "Gentiles." I realize that many liberal Christians try to argue that Paul does not maintain this exclusivist theology but I find their arguments unconvincing. On the other hand, it should be mentioned that while Paul thought he was writing letters, it is the claim of the conservative Christians that he was carving out dogmas. Paul never canonized his own convictions nor did he call his epistles scripture.

But to the question of whether or not Paul maintained an exclusivist theology, I would respond in the affirmative. I do not, however, conclude that exclusivist theology is the only legitimate Christian theology today. Finding myself unwilling and unable to manipulate the Pauline text into an inclusivist position, I am constrained to argue that Paul's polemical formulation was simply wrong. This should not be too startling an admission for any liberal Christian not bound to an inerrant view of scripture. Paul can be judged wrong about many things: his views on women and marriage, his limited understanding of slavery, his bias against homosexuality. Why then can he not be judged wrong in his exclusivist formulation of faith? He can still be right, even magnificently so, in his ecstatic expression of a covenanted life with God in Jesus. And yet he can be wrong, tragically wrong, in his inability to understand and appreciate other covenanted lives with God not based on the Christ event.

I find it unfruitful to argue from what Paul might say if he were part of this contemporary debate. We do not have Paul two thousand years later. What we do have is a reliable text of some seven or eight letters almost certainly written by Paul. All Christians agree that we must begin with this text. The division between the so-called liberals and conservatives is based on whether or not we end with the text. The conservative position is obviously simpler: if something is found in the text, the discussion is over. The liberal position is forever committed to pushing beyond the text, since liberal theology takes history seriously and believes that the final word has not yet been spoken. All of this is consistent with the theological developments we traced in Rosenzweig who continues to be our guide.

Can liberal and conservative Christians dialogue about this? Probably not. It is possible for liberals to understand that conservatives choose to follow Paul in his exclusivist theology, and it might even be possible for liberals to respect that choice, even though they think it is a wrong one. Certainly liberals have no problem in recognizing people who do make that choice as Christians, for fundamentalists, too, trust God because of what he has done in Jesus. But none of these premises is reciprocal. Conservative Christians cannot respect the position of liberals who choose to separate themselves from an exclusivist theology nor can they really recognize them as Christians. Exclusivist positions are nondialogical by definition. Conservative

Christians may enter into a discussion with liberal Christians but such discussion does not meet the criteria for dialogue that Rosenzweig would demand: the ability to respond from the dialogical character of the moment and not from a preformulated position, the willingness to be changed, the recognition that one's perspective is indeed a perspective, the realization that truth is beyond articulation and that revelation transcends propositional formulation.

Paul could have developed a dual covenant theology, but he didn't. He also could have lived his life within the Jesus Movement, a messianic Jewish sect requiring Gentiles to become members of a community centered in the Torah, but he didn't. He even could have anticipated the way of Marcion, which Robin Lane Fox describes in his monumental *Pagans and Christians*:

> At Rome in the 140s, the recent convert Marcion shocked the Church by denying any connection between the Gods of the Old and New Testament. By rewriting Scripture, he presented a powerful case. The Creator, he argued, was an incompetent being: why else had he afflicted women with the agonies of childbirth? "God" in the Old Testament was a "committed barbarian" who favored bandits and such terrorists as Israel's King David. Christ, by contrast, was the new and separate revelation of an altogether higher God.[62]

Marcion saw himself as a disciple of Paul and included Paul's epistles in his much-abbreviated biblical canon. Paul, of course, did not consciously father Marcion nor did he intend to foster a path based on total rejection of the Jewish heritage.

Paul rejected these three options: dual covenant theology, the Jesus Movement, and the total repudiation of his former Judaism. What he chose was the flawed synthesis which becomes Christianity. Not flawed in any lack of capacity to express its own spiritual center, but unsuccessful in articulating the relationship to the parent religion. Thus the resulting ambivalence which we have seen: good news for the Gentiles as recipients of a covenanted life and bad news for the Jews as enemies of that same faith, Jews whose existence is somehow necessary to the Christian end-time vision but Jews who must lose their essential Jewishness to be finally acceptable.

Despite this fundamental flaw in Paul's synthesis, it merits our full attention. It provides us with the canonical material Christian theologians are wrestling with to this day. It is the mother lode from which all the theological documents we considered earlier in this chapter were mined. Finally, it is the context in which any contribution from Rosenzweig to Jewish-Christian dialogue must be considered.

Paul's position is a theological *toũr de force*. His problem is to avoid the tack later taken by Marcion, who abandons the Torah, and yet not be forced to ally himself with the members of the Jesus Movement who observe the Torah. How can he find a middle way between the horns of this dilemma? Paul is saying that the Torah is the revelation of the only true God and yet he is also claiming that its observance is neither necessary for the Gentile members of his communities nor salvific for the Jewish members. Jewish Christians, in other words, may observe the Torah but with two reservations: that they do not consider that observance to be the source of their salvation and that they do not conclude that Torah observance gives them a higher status in the community than the Gentile members who neglect it.

Paul begins with an appeal to the fact that Jews existed before the Torah. "What then shall we say about Abraham, our forefather according to the flesh?" (Romans 4:1) What Paul says, of course, is that Abraham was God-centered without benefit of the Torah. He lived, after all, several centuries before the Sinai event. How could Abraham be God-centered before the Torah was revealed? Because of his faith, his trust in

God. Further in this same chapter, Paul argues that
this God-centeredness came even before the commandment of circumcision. With these premises in place,
Paul can move to his conclusion: Abraham, then, can
be the father of a God-centered community that is not
Torah observant, either regarding circumcision or any
other prescription of *halacha*.

Paul developed his point by presenting an unneces-
sary disjunction. If we agree with him that Abraham
entered into a right relationship with God because of
his faith and not because of the observance of the
Torah, then we are asked to choose between that faith
and Torah observance. Chapter 4, verse 14 capsulizes
that argument: "If it is the adherents of the law who
are to be the heirs, faith is null and the promise is
void." Paul's letter is not cast in dialogical form. The
Jewish community is not given a chance to respond.
Given such an opportunity, the illegitimacy of the
disjunction could have been exposed.

Why do we have to choose between faith and the
Torah? Jews do not believe that they become God-centered by observing the Torah, without at the same time
recognizing its character as gift and trusting the divine
Giver. That is the very meaning of *Matan Torah*, the
gift of the Torah. The Torah is Judaism's grace.
Living the Torah constitutes a faithful, grace-full, and
grateful response. Why does Paul try to separate what
God has put together? Here Paul wants us to choose
between faith and observance of the Law; later he will
want us to choose between the Jews and "the new
Israel." Why should we be forced to an either-or
response where a both-and possibility looms so large?

Once one accepts this disjunctive statement of the
argument, then the options are severely limited. It is
difficult to argue for faithless circumcision over faithful
trust in the living God. It is hard to defend confidence
in empty works over acceptance of God's grace. It is
impossible to choose flawless observance, with no
possibility of sin and repentance, as the basis of one's
confidence, over against openness to forgiveness offered

in Jesus' blood. And yet, all of these positions derive their power from the disjunctive framework in which they are presented. When that is removed, the whole strength of the argument collapses.

Jews can trust in the God of Abraham and acknowledge that the God of Moses is the same God. They can recognize the Torah as God's grace to Israel. They can live a Torah-observant life with gratitude and joy. Paul so easily forgets the *Simchat Torah*, the rejoicing in the Torah, so central to Jewish life. Furthermore, despite Paul, Jews can sin and yet have confidence in the God who forgives them their transgressions. Judaism constitutes a total and complete religious entity, with no need for Paul's good news or for Paul's Messiah.

One of the basic problems of religious dialogue is the inability of so many to think within the religious framework of their dialogical partners. Christians often ask how Jews can reject Jesus. How difficult it is for Christians to understand that most Jews don't reject Jesus so much as find him totally irrelevant. Christians might ask themselves how many sleepless nights they have spent wondering about the validity of God's revelations to Muhammad. It doesn't require much introspection for most Christians to realize that they function religiously without any serious attention to the claims of this third Abrahamite faith. Why then is it so difficult to understand that Jews can live with the same benign neglect of Christ?

Now one might argue that this suggested polemic is a distortion of Paul, since he argues that Abraham is the Father "of all who believe without being circumcised" (Romans 4:11), but also "of the circumcised who are not merely circumcised but also follow the example of the faith which our father Abraham had before he was circumcised." (Romans 4:12) In other words, could Paul be claiming that God is the father of Jews and Christians alike? Unfortunately not. The development of the letter makes it clear that he is referring to Gentile Christians and Christians of Jewish origin like himself.

Paul destroys any possibility of a dual covenant theology when he writes that "Christ is the end of the law, that every one who has faith may be justified." (Romans 10:4)   Understanding the double meaning of *end* as fulfillment or termination does not alleviate the force of this judgement.   There was God-centeredness before the giving of the Torah, as we see in the lives of the patriarchs; there was God-centeredness during the time of the Torah's validity, from Moses to Christ; now there is God-centeredness without the Torah and this is available to Jewish and Gentile Christian alike.

Paul clarifies this point in his letter to the Galatians:

> Now before faith came, we were confined under the law, kept under restraint until faith should be revealed, so that the law was our custodian until Christ came, that we might be justified by faith. But now that faith has come, we are no longer under a custodian; for in Christ Jesus you are all sons of God, through faith. (Galatians 3:23-26)

The Torah's role was provisional and temporary. This enables Paul both to recognize the Torah as God-given and good (thereby avoiding the later error of Marcion) and yet deny its ongoing validity within the new community of faith (thus separating himself from the "Judaizers" he opposes so vigorously). It also eschews the both-and option of two valid covenantal communities and necessitates the understanding of Christianity as the true Israel and the consequent rejection of Judaism.

In a recent conversation with an Orthodox Jewish friend, I was struck by his argument that Christianity's basic problem for him stems from its perpetual claim to be a deeper living of the Torah juxtaposed with its rejection of Torah observance. This, of course, is the legacy of Paul. No matter how friendly Christianity seems towards much of its Jewish heritage, its interpretation of the Torah as a provisional and limited expression of God's dealing with Israel forever separates the daughter religion from its parent. I see no alternative but to embrace the separateness but in such a way as to leave the integrity of the Jewish covenant untouched. Yes, Christianity means trusting God because of Jesus and living the covenant established in his name. This does not, however, constitute Christianity as the new Israel nor does this new covenant replace an old one. As Rosenzweig so often argued, there are two covenant communities and they exist together in time until the end of history.

Jewish Blindness

Retaining God as the author of the Torah but limiting the time of its validity seemed to solve one problem for Paul, however many problems it created for future generations of Christians and Jews down to our own day. Paul still had to face the apparent obduracy of his former co-religionists in accepting his good news. There were, of course, converts from Judaism to Paul's Christianity but, for the most part, the Jewish community continued to trust God because of Sinai, not because of Jesus.

Paul had to understand this failure of his own people to receive his message. His answer consisted of attributing to the Jews a combination of blindness and provocation to jealousy. Paul bases the blindness charge on a bizarre interpretation of Exodus 34. The passage occurs in the context of Moses communicating God's message to the people. Each time Moses went into God's presence, he returned with shining face. The people were disturbed by this, so Moses developed a simple solution: a veil. We are told in verses 33-35 of this chapter that:

When Moses had finished speaking with them, he put a veil on his face; but whenever Moses went in before the Lord to speak with him, he took the veil off, until he came out; and when he came out, and told the people of Israel what he was commanded, the people of Israel saw the face of Moses, that the skin of Moses' face shone; and Moses would put the veil upon his face again until he went in to speak with him.

Though not pellucid, the point seems to be that Moses did not use the veil either when he was talking with God or with the people, but he did use the veil at other times so that he would be less intimidating.

Twice Paul develops a midrash on this passage, once in 2 Corinthians and once in Romans. In the former letter, Paul first contrasts the two dispensations. The Torah was written on tablets of stone and it was the dispensation of death. (2 Corinthians 3:7) And yet, even this provisional and far from perfect covenant "came with such splendor that the Israelites could not look at Moses' face because of its brightness, fading as it was . . ." (2 Corinthians 3:7) The new dispensation of the Spirit (also called the dispensation of righteousness) will be attended with greater splendor. (2 Corinthians 3:8-9) As a matter of fact, the old dispensation "has come to have no splendor at all" (2 Corinthians 3:10) for it has now faded away and been replaced.

What does this have to do with the veil? Paul writes that Moses "had put a veil over his face so that the Israelites might not see the end of the fading splendor." (2 Corinthians 3:12) And Jews who "to this day" read the Torah have a veil over their minds, unless they abandon that now outmoded and surpassed "old covenant" and turn to the new dispensation preached by Paul. In an excellent article on this subject, the Jewish scholar Michael Cook points out that these accusations of blindness block dialogue because they portray the other party as "impervious to

obvious truth" and raise "the possibility that such opaqueness is a permanent condition."[63]
This presumption of blindness, of course, is carried on into subsequent Christian iconography and, more importantly, into Christian consciousness. It constitutes part of the patronizing arrogance of Christians who talk to Jews realizing full well that these people are closed to the "obvious truth" of Christ. This is an unavoidable consequence of the exclusivist position, since it cannot in principle entertain the option that it might be wrong or indeed that its beliefs are *an* interpretation, *a* perspective, *a* point of view.

In Romans, Paul quotes Isaiah and the Psalms in describing the blind and darkened eyes of the Jews. (Romans 11: 7 & 8)   But here the blindness is connected to a purpose, other than the mere boast of the superiority of Paul's revelational experience in Christ. This blindness which causes so many Jews to resist Paul's message allows Gentiles to come into the covenant community. The breaking off of the original olive branches permits wild olive branches to be grafted onto the olive tree. Nevertheless, the original branches can always be re-grafted. (Romans 11:17-23)   For Paul believes that this combination of an inrush of new converts among the circumcised is but the paradoxical veil hiding a divine mystery. Gentile enthusiasm and Jewish blindness will yet serve God's deeper purposes. The Gentile Christians must remain humble and Paul must remain hopeful, for the Jews will be provoked to jealousy when they see salvation coming to "Gentile sinners" and a great Jewish ingathering will occur in the wake of that event.

There is both poignancy and pathos in Paul's attempt to bring together these two disparate dimensions of his gospel: his exclusivist salvational position and the unwillingness of most Jews to accept it. "Israel failed to obtain what it sought. The elect obtained it, but the rest were hardened..." (Romans 11:7)   Paul loves his people too much to understand that hardening as resulting in the destruction that long ago had come to

Pharaoh when his heart was hardened. This hardening must have a purpose in God's plan. "So I ask, have they stumbled so as to fall? By no means! But through their trespass salvation has come to the Gentiles, so as to make Israel jealous." (Romans 11:11) Not only does this explain God's larger salvific plan, not only does it explicate the blindness of so many Jews, not only does it serve as a reminder to Gentile Christians not to lord it over Jewish Christians, but also it provides us with the key to Paul's own urgent mission: "I magnify my ministry in order to make my fellow Jews jealous, and thus save some of them." (Romans 11:13-14)

There is much to be said for this argument formulated around 57 C.E. It enables Paul to bring together in one great hope various facets of what he knows and believes. There is only one path of salvation. The glorious return of Jesus is not too far away. The Jewish people are especially beloved to God. The Gentiles are responding to the gospel more than the Jews. How magnificently all of this flows together in his hoped for scenario of God's future. Even if Paul is wrong in this formulation, and I believe he is, one cannot but admire his genius.

As in the former case where Paul was able both to deny the Torah's ongoing validity and yet accept its divine authorship, here too Paul seems to have it both ways. He can portray the Jews as blind in clinging to "the old dispensation" and yet recognize their part in the ultimate salvific plan of God. Either now or later, the Jews must cease to be Jews and become Christians. In other words, they must cease to trust what God revealed at Sinai as having abiding validity and entrust their lives to the new covenant revealed in Jesus. An ingenious but ultimately unsuccessful solution.

Why do I assert that this solution is flawed? First, because the glorious return of Jesus did not occur as soon as Paul seems to have anticipated. Second, because the mass conversion of Jews also did not take place. Third, because the problem Paul was attempting to solve is a pseudo-problem which dissolves as soon as one abandons the polemical exclusivity Paul brings to its analysis. Fourth, because Paul's solution ultimately entails what, from a Jewish viewpoint, constitutes unfaithfulness. Paul can praise the Jews endlessly for their heritage but the final truth about them is that they are abandoned to a religion that has been essentially bankrupt since the coming of Christ. The only solution Paul offers them is to drop their religious identity and accept a new identity as Christians.

To claim that they continue to be Jews and that their Judaism is somehow completed when they deny their own covenantal reality is a distortion of dialogue that has no place in serious efforts to improve Jewish-Christian understanding. A Jew who becomes a Christian is no more a completed Jew than a Christian who becomes a Muslim is a completed Christian. What we are talking about is conversion, and according to Paul's explicit teaching in Romans, the only real choice Jews have in the matter is whether to be converted now or later, since the scenario necessitates their conversion at some point.

Christians have never lacked imagination in discussing this process--Duns Scotus, an otherwise reputable medieval theologian, thought that most Jews could be killed, as long as a few were kept in Wales to be on hand for the finale in which they were publicly to convert to Christianity before history's end. This is not too much more obscene than the harassment many Jews experience today at the hands of their fundamentalist "friends" who want them to go to live in Israel so that the end-time drama, which involves their mass conversion, might be hastened to its climax.

If dialogue entails allowing the other party to define itself, then, as Michael Cook points out, "the reality has to be grappled with that, what Paul construes to be blindness, Jews consider to be their *clearsightedness*."[64] Rosenzweig's guidelines allow for this kind of dialogue. Anything short of them permits little more than polite discussions. There are those who are willing to pursue an agenda for Jewish-Christian understanding that allows for Christian exclusivist theology with its consequent missionary imperative. Jews willing to engage in discussions within those parameters are certainly deserving of respect. I see such conversations, however, as holding little hope of moving us towards a future of substantive dialogue.

Beyond Paul

I share Michael Cook's hope that "we seek to combine with one another in our separately achieved perceptions of when God has been most manifest in past history, merging the results of our discoveries, pooling rather than polarizing our representations of truth."[65] This hope, of course, already breathes the air of Rosenzweig's meaning of dialogue. It speaks of perceptions of God's manifestation in history, of discoveries, and of representations of truth. But perceptions, discoveries, and representations describe a modern world view, one allowing for more than one true religion, more than one way of trusting the God who continues to covenant with humankind in surprising ways.

Ends and beginnings connect in theological discourse. Beginning with contemporary expressions of the dialogue emerging between Jews and Christians, we were led back to Paul, the first articulate Christian. Paul's writings are canonical, so there can be no Christian theology which does not begin with them. What is important in our understanding of the current status of Jewish-Christian dialogue is that we not end with them. I see only three paths for our future: the old polemics and prejudices, the discussions based on Christianity's continued exclusivist theology of salvation, and the new path opened up by Franz Rosenzweig.

The first option is nothing more than the old ignorance, leading eventually to further bloodshed and tears. The second option is possible and is found in clear form in conservative Christian theology and in veiled form in most mainstream theology as well. The third path has little official expression at this point in the Christian world and minimal recognition in the Jewish community. It embodies the essential insights of Rosenzweig regarding the noncognitional character of revelation and the consequent possibility of two true religions, two authentic covenantal communities, each of which is faithful to the God of Abraham. It is here that I most feel the fresh breezes of the future. It is here that I believe the next generation of Jewish-Christian dialogue can find its most fruitful workplace.

I know no better guide than Franz Rosenzweig to help us meet this challenge at this growing edge of Jewish-Christian dialogue today. The response to which he calls Christians is three-fold: the rejection of all inerrancy theories about scripture, the renunciation of all exclusivist truth or salvational claims, and a witness to faith accompanied by an openness to inter-faith.

Scripture contains countless errors--historical, geographical, etymological, geological, sociological--but it also contains one great truth, a true witness to the presence of the Divine in human history and directions for trusting that Ultimate Reality in building the earth and a human community of justice, compassion, and peace. The Hebrew Bible opens up that path of faith in terms of many covenantal experiences but, most importantly, in the Exodus story and the subsequent covenant of Sinai. That was enough, is enough, and will always be enough for a total religious existence. The Christian Testament discloses that path of faith in terms of the person of Jesus. That too was, is, and will always be sufficient for a complete spiritual life. In that sense, these two paths of faith are inerrant. Living the Torah and living in Christ will infallibly lead people to *shalom*, to a relational fullness with the Divine and with the human.

The biblical revelational traditions do not justify exclusivist claims. Let us reject such claims once and for all. As much as they serve our human insecurities, they must be gracefully surrendered. Long ago a divine oracle in Amos pointed out that God has other stories than his story with Israel. Is this not the God who not only brought Israel up from the land of Egypt but also "the Philistines from Caphtor and the Syrians from Kir?" (Amos 9:7) By the same token, Christians need to reexamine the words attributed to Jesus in John's gospel: "I am the way, and the truth, and the life; no one comes to the Father, but by me." (John 14:6) "Coming to the Divine through Jesus" refers to the consciousness of all who are receptive to God as a child to a loving parent. That consciousness can be found in a Jew as much as in a Christian.

With the two stumbling blocks of inerrancy and exclusivism removed, Jews and Christians can meet at a level of dialogue hinted at in Rosenzweig's correspondence with Ehrenberg. We can respond to the hopes that Michael Cook has expressed so eloquently. We can anticipate with Rosemary Ruether a Christianity that can be a good news without being a bad news for Jews. We can work together as partners in faith in a world that has all but forgotten how to trust the Divine. We can reach out to the spiritually homeless without the rancor of polemics and competition. We can serve and preserve the garden Earth, fulfilling the co-creative mandate given to us in our shared biblical account of humankind's creation.[66]

CHAPTER FIVE

Notes

1. The first volume, *Discerning the Way*, was published by Seabury Press in 1980. In this 201-page work, other than Jesus and Paul, no one is cited more frequently than Franz Rosenzweig. The second volume, *A Christian Theology of the People Israel*, and a third volume, *Christ in Context*, have been published by Harper & Row in 1987 and 1988, respectively. A fourth volume, *The Covenant and the World*, is projected at the time of this writing.

2. van Buren, *A Christian Theology of the People Israel*, p.1

3. van Buren, *A Christian Theology of the People Israel*, p.9.

4. This is from his article, "A Jewish Viewpoint on *Nostra Aetate*," appearing in *Twenty Years of Jewish-Catholic Relations*, edited by Eugene Fisher, James Rudin, and Marc Tanenbaum. (New York: Paulist Press, 1986), p. 54.

5. Mark Smith discusses this in terms of the Catholic Lectionary in his article in *Fireball and the Lotus*, edited by Ronald H. Miller and James B. Kenney. (Santa Fe, NM: Bear and Company, 1987), pp. 56-64.

6. This is a central theme of Rosemary Radford Ruether's provocative study, *Faith and Fratricide*. (New York: Seabury Press, 1974).

7. These are quoted, for example, in Rabbi Falk's enlightening book on the Jewishness of Jesus.

Harvey Falk, *Jesus the Pharisee*. (New York, Paulist Press, 1985), p. 15.

8. This is quoted by Rabbi Hershel Matt in his article, "How Shall A Believing Jew View Christianity?" appearing in Judaism, Fall, 1975, p. 392.

9. This is from Maimonides' letter to Hasdai Ha-Levi as quoted in *A Maimonides Reader* edited by Isadore Twersky. (New York: Behrman House Inc., 1972), p. 478.

10. Falk, *Jesus the Pharisee*, p. 15.

11. An extraordinarily successful example of this can be found in Rabbi Yechiel Eckstein's *What Christians Should Know About Jews and Judaism*. (Wayco, TX: Word Publishers, 1984).

12. A good overview of the work of these and other theologians can be found in "New Trends in Catholic Religious Thought," by John Pawlikowski in Fisher, et al, Nostra Aetate, pp. 169-190.

13. *The New York Times National News*, Wednesday, July 1, 1987, "Church Affirms Validity of Judaism" by Ari L. Goldman, p. 8. This was subsequently published in the minutes of the Sixteenth General Synod of the United Church of Christ, June 25-30, 1987, pp. 67 and 68. Both the Episcopal Church and the Presbyterian Church have made similar statements in 1988 rejecting replacement theology or what is sometimes called *supersessionism*. Rosemary Ruether strongly concurs: "The supersessionary pattern of Christian faith distorts both Jewish and Christian reality. We should think rather of Judaism and Christianity as parallel paths, flowing from common memories in Hebrew scripture, which are then reformulated into separate ways that lead two peoples to formulate the

dialectic of past and future through different historical experiences. But the dilemma of foretaste and hope remains the same for both. For both live in the same reality of incompleted human existence itself." *Disputed Questions* (Maryknoll, New York: Orbis Books, 1989), p. 71.

14. Thomas Merton, *A Vow of Conversation: Journals 1964-1965*, edited and with a preface by Naomi Burton Stone. (New York: Farrar, Straus, Giroux, 1988), p. 76. A few months earlier, on July 13, 1964, Heschel travelled to the Trappist monastery in Gethsemane, Kentucky, to visit Merton. They spoke about one of the earlier and bolder proposals for a conciliar document, one that was discarded along the path of political compromise. Merton writes in his journal entry the next day: "Heschel thinks that the Jewish Chapter will never be accepted by the Vatican Council. We spoke of how symbolic this fact was. In my opinion, the acceptance of this Chapter and the consequent implicit act of repentance is necessary for the Church. In reality, the Church stands to benefit more by it than the Jews." p. 63.

15. Even at the time of this final reading of the text, I find on page 3, Section I of the *Chicago Tribune* today, March 12, 1989 that in a four-day summit meeting with the American archbishops, Pope John Paul II's parting message was: "We are guardians of something given . . . something which is not the result of reflection, however competent, on cultural and social questions of the day, and is not merely the best path among many, but the one and only path to salvation."

16. *Tanakh* is an acronym constituted by the first letters (T-N-K) of the three parts of the Hebrew Bible: the Torah, the Neviim (Prophets), and the Ketuvim (Writings). "Old Testament," of course,

implies the superceding value of a "New" Testament. Consequently, I use the terms Hebrew Bible and Christian Testament in this book.

17. Abbott (ed), *The Documents of Vatican II*, p. 664.

18. Abbott (ed), *The Documents of Vatican II*, p. 644.

19. Abbott (ed), *The Documents of Vatican II*, p.665.

20. Eugene Fischer, et al. *Twenty Years of Jewish-Catholic Relations*, p. 52.

21. Abbott (ed), *The Documents of Vatican II*, p. 667.

22. Abbott (ed), *The Documents of Vatican II*, p. 658.

23. Abbott (ed), *The Documents of Vatican II*, p. 667.

24. Abbott (ed), *The Documents of Vatican II*, p. 664.

25. It is an interesting commentary on Jewish-Christian relations that the copy I am using was printed by the Midwest Regional Office of the Anti-Defamation League of B'nai B'rith: Chicago, 1975. It is also available, of course, through the U.S. Catholic Conference Office of Publishing and Promotion Services: Washington, D.C..

26. "Guidelines and Suggestions for Implementing the Conciliar Declaration *Nostra Aetate*." p. 1.

27. "Guidelines and Suggestions for Implementing the Conciliar Declaration *Nostra Aetate*." p.2.

28. Pawlikowski's article in Fisher, et al, *Twenty Years of Jewish-Catholic Relations*, p. 185.

29. "Guidelines and Suggestions for Implementing the Conciliar Declaration *Nostra Aetate*," p. 2.

30. "Guidelines and Suggestions for Implementing the Conciliar Declaration *Nostra Aetate*," p. 3.

31. "Guidelines and Suggestions for Implementing the Conciliar Declaration *Nostra Aetate*," p. 4.

32. Fisher, et al, *Twenty Years of Jewish-Catholic Relations*, p. 213. This document is also found on pp. 33-36 in a summary of papal statements entitled *Pope John Paul II on Jews and Judaism 1979-1986*, with Introduction and Commentary by the editors, Eugene J. Fisher and Leon Klenicki (Washington, D.C.: United States Catholic Conference, 1987).

33. Fisher, et al, *Twenty Years of Jewish-Catholic Relations*, p. 213.

34. Fisher, et al, *Twenty Years of Jewish-Catholic Relations*, p. 213.

35. Fisher, et al, *Twenty Years of Jewish-Catholic Relations*, p. 214.

36. Fisher, et al, *Twenty Years of Jewish-Catholic Relations*, p. 214.

37. Fisher, et al, *Twenty Years of Jewish-Catholic Relations*, p. 216.

38. Fisher, et al, *Twenty Years of Jewish-Catholic Relations*, p. 216. Emphasis my own.

39. Fisher, et al, *Twenty Years of Jewish-Catholic Relations*, p. 216.

40. Fisher, et al, *Twenty Years of Jewish-Catholic Relations*, p. 216.

41. Fisher, et al, *Twenty Years of Jewish-Catholic Relations*, p. 216.

42. Fisher, et al, *Twenty Years of Jewish-Catholic Relations*, p. 217.

43. This document is found in Helga Croner's *More Stepping Stones To Jewish-Christian Relations: An Unabridged Collection of Christian Documents 1975-1983* (New York: Paulist Press, 1985), pp. 220-232. This is a second volume following her earlier *Stepping Stones to Further Jewish-Christian Relations* of 1977.

44. On October 18, 1977 when the bishops were gathered in Rome for the Synod on "catechetics in our time," the proceedings were so disappointing to many liberal theologians that Cardinal Willebrands made a written intervention on "Catechetics and Judaism," a refreshing corrective to the otherwise reactionary meeting. This document is found in *More Stepping Stones*, pp. 56-59.

45. *More Stepping Stones*, p. 222. The italics are in the text.

46. *More Stepping Stones*, pp. 224. Whether this sentiment will result in a reform of the present lectionary is questionable.

47. *More Stepping Stones*, p. 225.

48. *More Stepping Stones*, p. 226.

49. *More Stepping Stones*, p. 223.

50. *More Stepping Stones*, p. 223.

51. *More Stepping Stones,* p. 223. It should be noted that Cardinal Willebrands is president of the commission that produced the document. The presence of so much language that he would reject is a further indication of the decline of the reform tradition originally encouraged by Pope John XXIII's calling of the Second Vatican Council.

52. This position is exceptionally well argued in Lloyd Gaston's *Paul and the Torah* (Vancouver: University of British Columbia Press, 1987).

53. "But when Cephas came to Antioch, I opposed him to his face. . . ." (Galatians 2:11) "And there arose a sharp contention, so that they [Paul and Barabas] separated from each other. . . ." (Acts 15:39)

54. Rosenzweig, on p. 412 of *The Star of Redemption* calls him "the first theologian of the new religion." If a theologian is a systematic thinker, then this claim may be exaggerated. Paul's ideas are insightful and brilliant but lack the structured elegance of a theological system.

55. *Halacha,* derived from the Jewish word for *walk,* refers to Jewish law. For an interesting discussion of the relationship of *halacha* to *aggada* (the story tradition) in Judaism and Christianity, see Rabbi Marc Gellman's article, "Law and Story in Judaism and Christianity," in *Fireball and the Lotus,* pp. 65-72.

56. It is important to distinguish the legitimacy of these original messianic Jews from the various groups claiming such identity today. First of all, today's Jews for Jesus or Messianic Jews are conservative Christians. They are not centered in the Torah nor do they consider it to have ongoing salvific meaning. Their use of the word "Jew" is thus both a deception and an insult to Jews and

Christians alike. See the excellent treatment of this movement in Yechiel Eckstein's *What Christians Should Know about Jews and Judaism*, p. 287-299.

57. It is common in dialogical contexts to use B.C.E. (Before the Common Era) and C.E. (the Common Era) instead of the Christian confessional terms B.C. (Before Christ) and A.D. (*Anno Domini*, in the Year of the Lord).

58. Rosenzweig, *Briefe und Tagebücher*, I-2 pp. 799-800. Translation my own.

59. Fackenheim, *What is Judaism?* p. 112.

60. Originally found in Habakkuk 2:4, Paul quotes this text both in Romans 1:17 and Galatians 3:11.

61. For an understanding of the place of Evangelical Christians in contemporary religious America, see my article, "A Roadmap to Religious America," pp. 13-31 in *Fireball and the Lotus*. For a Jewish perspective on the Religious Right, see Yechiel Eckstein's article in the same volume, "A Jewish Perspective on the Religious Right," pp. 32-55.

62. Alfred A. Knopf, Inc., New York, 1987, p. 332.

63. "The Ties that Bind: An Exposition of II Corinthians 3:12-4:6 and Romans 11:7-10" in *When Jews and Christians Meet*, edited by Jakob J. Petuchowski. [Albany, New York: State University of New York Press, 1988] p. 126.

64. *When Jews and Christians Meet*, edited by Jakob J. Petuchowski, p. 136, emphasis is his.

65. *When Jews and Christians Meet*, edited by Jakob J. Petuchowski, p. 137.

66. Genesis 2:15.   See Helen Kenik's excellent article on this text, "Towards a Biblical Basis for Creation Theology," pp. 27-75 in *Western Spririituality*, ed. by Matthew Fox (Notre Dame, IN: Fides, 1979).

A DAY OF DIALOGUE

On November 4, 1979 close to the fiftieth anniversary of Franz Rosenzweig's death, Common Ground, an adult education center for interfaith study and dialogue, hosted a program entitled "Franz Rosenzweig: New Birth of Jewish-Christian Dialogue." The program was co-sponsored by Congregation Solel, a Reform community in Highland Park, Illinois. The keynote address was delivered by Professor Nahum N. Glatzer, former student of Rosenzweig and one of the foremost exponents of his thought. Dr. Glatzer also worked closely with Martin Buber, succeeding to Buber's chair at the University of Frankfurt. Dr. Glatzer is Emeritus Professor of Jewish History at Brandeis University and one of the most prolific authors in the field of Judaica. He was introduced by Rabbi Robert J. Marx of Congregation Solel. Rabbi Marx and I were respondents to the address.

The following text is an edited transcript of Dr. Glatzer's address:

My topic today is: Yom Kippur 1913. This is a story which concerns Franz Rosenzweig, one of the great Jewish religious thinkers of this century. It is a story about his way to Judaism from a nonobservant adherence to the Jewish faith which characterized his family, a well-to-do family living in Kassel, Germany. The Rosenzweigs never denied their belonging to the Jewish community but did little to affirm their Judaism. Franz Rosenzweig grew up with no real knowledge of his Judaism with the exception of his experience with his uncle, Adam Rosenzweig, an artist who lived in the

Rosenzweig home.   His uncle, on the day
Franz began school, held the boy in his arms
and said emphatically:

> "My boy, you are going among
> people for the first time today;
> remember as long as you live
> that you are a Jew."

That's all. It's an amazing thing because no
more was needed in order to preserve in this
boy the feeling that to belong to Judaism, to
be a Jew, was somehow very important.
    He knew very well what Christianity
was. At one point in his letters he said:

> "We live in a Christian world,
> in a Christian civilization; we
> are   raised   on   Christian
> literature, and all that is
> Christian. What is Jewish that
> lasts? This means that Judaism
> doesn't really exist anymore; it's
> very   good   to   belong   to   a
> community which has this kind
> of a history but does it mean I
> have to do something about it?
> The answer is: 'No.'"

He also had friends, most off whom were of
Jewish   origin,   who   were   converts   to
Christianity.
    But Franz Rosenzweig in his early years at
the university was not bothered by this whole
problem of "Am I a Jew?"   "Am I a potential
Christian?"   He studied, first medicine and then
history and philosophy, his real interests. At one
point there arose in his heart and in the hearts of
some of his friends and converted relatives the
question, "Is that all we have, all we need -- our

understanding of nineteenth century German history and the progression of civilization from the Far East to the Near East to the southern part of Europe, into Prussia, into Berlin, culminating (if I may exaggerate a little bit) in the lecture room of Professor Hegel?"

Hegel was the great philosopher of history, the highly admired academician in the newly established University of Berlin at the beginning of the nineteenth century. He taught his students that what the individual suffers is unimportant. If an individual perishes, it doesn't matter too much. It is painful for the family and maybe for the town, but what matters is the community at large and humanity at large. We are talking about *Menschheit* (humanity), not the individual. We cannot, as philosophers, concern ourselves with the fate or destiny of the individual. The individual perishes and that's all right, because then we create space for a new generation of human beings.

Franz Rosenzweig and his friends challenged these Hegelian concepts. "That cannot be; it cannot be true that I and you, my friends, do not matter. I was born; I grow up; I suffer; I love; I hate; one day I'll die. Is this not important? It must be." Philosophy doesn't answer this question, especially Idealistic philosophy in Germany which goes back to Greek philosophy, back to Plato. There the individual does not matter. Franz Rosenzweig decided that we have to look for some context where the individual does matter. And that context is religion.

Religion concerns itself with the individual who is not an interchangeable unit. We cannot say, "If we don't have X, then we have Y, we have Z, maybe somebody will be here to continue. The individual doesn't matter." Of course there is the religious community and there should be; but a community is composed of individuals. And God, if we may use this concept freely, is interested in each and every human soul. That is the idea of religion, in both Judaism and Christianity. The individual is actually indivisible, irreplaceable, and loved, not by the state, but by God.

Rosenzweig went a step further to declare Protestantism such a religion, and in a wider sense, Christianity. He knew Christianity very well; he had made notes on his readings in early Christian philosophy and theology and on early medieval Christian thought. He knew Augustine and other Church theologians thoroughly. In his thinking he was becoming Christianized. So it seemed natural that he, having come to share the views of his Jewish Christian friends, decided to become a Christian.

A broadly and deeply educated young man of twenty-seven, Rosenzweig found himself engaged in nightly discussions with these same friends during the summer of 1913. He was trying to resolve personal questions arising from his intellectual decision to become a Christian. How can a modern European intellectual accept a religious outlook, a religion which is actually practiced by the masses of Europe? Christianity, although it may address itself to the intellectual, is in the main a religion of the masses. The symbolism of Christianity is a mass symbolism and the language of Christianity is a language addressed to the masses. Can an intellectual, therefore, agree to it?

At this time Rosenzweig and his group were reading a currently popular novel in which the hero encountered many terrible situations; his world was falling to pieces. Franz Rosenzweig asked his friend, Eugene Rosenstock, "What would you do in such a situation?" Said Rosenstock, who was a professor of law in Leipzig, "I would go to the nearest church, fall to my knees, and pray."

That was a response which Rosenzweig did not expect from Rosenstock, highly educated yet using the simple language of a believer. That convinced Rosenzweig that if Rosenstock could do that, he could do it too. He was confirmed in his decision to become a Christian.

But he made this decision within himself. Approaching Yom Kippur, the Day of Atonement, in that year of 1913, Rosenzweig decided that he would like to enter the church as a Jew, just as St. Paul became a Christian as a Jew. Paul was a Jew up to the very moment that the voice addressed him, "Why do you persecute me?" (Acts 9:4) At that moment Paul radically changed his entire outlook and became a follower of Jesus and put himself at the disposal of the Master to be sent wherever the Master would send him.

As Rosenzweig's mother tells it, the family used to go three times a year to the temple to participate, perhaps that says too much, to be present at the worship. Rosenzweig went on Rosh Hashanah to the local synagogue in Kassel and departed feeling cold and left out. It was a performance where no one was really touched. The experience was meaningless for Franz Rosenzweig, who went to the synagogue knowing that these were his last days as a Jew. In a few weeks he would be a member of a Christian church.

He went home. His mother was a sensitive lady, very cultured and very much concerned with her only son. She said, "Dear Franz, I understand that you are planning to be baptized." He said, "Yes, Mother." Lifting up the New Testament he said, "This is the truth, Jesus." His mother replied, "But you were in the synagogue on Rosh Hashana." And he said, "Yes, and on Yom Kippur I will be in the synagogue again." To which statement his mother said, "No you won't. I won't let you in because there is no room for apostates in our synagogue."

Franz went to Berlin, which is not far from Kassel. He took a hotel room and then looked around for the nearest synagogue. He found a little orthodox synagogue. He went there to participate in the Kol Nidre service on the eve of Yom Kippur. That must have influenced him strongly. He came back the next morning and he stayed there the entire day of Yom Kippur. This is the mother's report, as given by her to the present speaker.

In the traditional Jewish ritual the service starts early in the morning and ends in the evening. Rosenzweig participated throughout the day, but nowhere in his later writings does he make explicit reference to his own experience that day, though he refers to the ceremonies and rituals of Yom Kippur in various writings.

It is a dramatic service, which starts out with the confession of sinfulness. "We have done wrong." *We*, not I personally, not you personally, but as a community, we have failed. Jews are very often aware of the fact that *we* would have perished long ago. There have been institutions directed against the Jewish community, but we survived. That is the feeling of the Jew throughout the year, but on Yom Kippur he realizes that, yes, he has survived, but he has failed as a human being. As a member of the community, as a member of humanity, he has done wrong. And he recites alphabetically, "We have sinned, we have done wrong, and we have transgressed . . ." 22 or 24 lines of transgressions, corresponding to the number of the letters of the alphabet; that confession is repeated several times during the day; again and again the community rises and confesses its failure before God.

Then comes the entreaty, the prayer for forgiveness. The Lord is a God of forgiveness and the community implores God to say, "I have forgiven." That is how the worship, the drama, the liturgy of Yom Kippur starts in the traditional service. Then the Torah is taken out of the Ark; Leviticus, Chapter 16, is read. What do you expect to hear from the Torah on this holiest day of the Jewish calendar? You hear about the organization of sacrificial worship in the time of the desert sanctuary and later in the time of the first temple in Jerusalem.

God tells Moses to speak to Aaron, telling him to take a young bullock for the sin offering and a ram for the burnt offering. The high priest should put on holy linen coats and linen breeches. He should wear a linen girdle and a linen maitre, for these are holy garments. Then he washes his body in water. The children of Israel take two kids for the sin offering, and one ram for the burnt offering. Aaron, the high priest, offers his bullock and makes atonement for himself and his house. Then two goats are chosen; lots are cast. One is for the Lord and the other is a scapegoat. Aaron brings the goat which is the Lord's and offers it as a sin offering; the other one, a scapegoat, is to make atonement, being led into the desert and released. Aaron then kills the bullock for the sin offering which is to make atonement for himself and his house. He takes the censer full of burning coal from the altar and his hands are full of sweet incense. He brings it within the veil of the sanctuary and he takes the blood of the bullock and sprinkles it with his fingers seven times. He then kills the goat as the sin offering for the people and brings its blood within the veil of the sanctuary, and makes atonement, and so it goes on . . . and that's just the beginning.

There is a very detailed description of the bullocks and the goats, how they are killed and brought as a sacrifice, of the priestly washing.

The high priest constantly takes a bath and puts on new garments for the next part of the ceremony. Ceremonious procedures are prescribed for this work of atonement. If the priest slaughters the bullock and takes the blood and sprinkles it seven times on the altar, it does the work of atonement. Was this still of any value to a man in 1913? Of course not. It is tradition to chant this chapter; but you cannot expect that this should apply to the congregations of Jews in 1913 or 1914 or in any other modern time.

But could it be of importance to a man like Franz Rosenzweig, who came there to see for the last time in his life what Judaism was? What he wanted was to experience the presence of God, which he knew he could experience in the church. There, in various forms, depending on whether you are Catholic or Protestant, there the presence of God is visible. In the community or in the celebration of the Mass, God manifests Himself and the worshipper experiences God's presence.

The reading from the Torah on Yom Kippur, like on any other Sabbath or holy day, is followed by the reading from the prophets; and the reading for this day is from Isaiah. There you see a different kind of Judaism. The community complains to the prophet Isaiah: "Why, when we fasted, did You not see? When we starved our bodies, did You pay no heed?" (Isaiah 58:3) And then the prophet answers as Isaiah 58 continues:

> Because you fast in strife and contention, and you strike with a wicked fist! Your fasting today is not such as to make your voice heard on high. Is such the fast I desire, a day for men to starve their bodies? Is it bowing the head like a bulrush and lying in sackcloth and ashes? Do you call that a fast, a day when the Lord is favor-

able? No, this is the fast I desire: to unlock the fetters of wickedness, and untie the cords of the yoke to let the oppressed go free; to break off every yoke. It is to share your bread with the hungry, and to take the wretched poor into your home; when you see the naked, to clothe him, and not to ignore your own kin. Then shall your light burst through like the dawn and your healing spring up quickly; your vindicator shall march before you, the Presence of the Lord shall be your rear guard. Then, when you call, the Lord will answer; when you cry, He will say: Here I am. If you banish the yoke from your midst, the menacing hand, the evil speech, and you offer your compassion to the hungry and satisfy the famished creature--then shall your light shine in darkness, and your gloom shall be like noonday.

(Isaiah 58:4-10)

A person may have followed all the rules of the ritual as the day demands, and yet not expect any kind of attention. What matters is to have done your duty towards your fellow human beings. There is a yoke upon the oppressed, and it is up to you to realize this yoke, to remove it. There is hunger in the world and it is your job to relieve this hunger, and so on. All these afflictions are your own afflictions. "You shall not hide your-self from your own flesh." Your neighbor is you. That means--you do it to yourself. Don't think that he is over there, and you can look away and he doesn't concern you. No. Your neighbor is your duty; he is you. Then the rituals may come in, and then you will be able to expect an answer from God. That's a different kind of scripture, a different kind of religion, and a different kind of relationship between God and us.

The reading goes on. In the afternoon prayer, the martyrs of Israel are remembered, the so-called ten martyrs in the Hadrianic persecution of the second century, the medieval martyrs, those persecuted during the Crusades, all of them are remembered.

You hear the melodies, the haunting, ancient melodies of Yom Kippur, repeated by the community. The worship of the high priest in the temple is recalled, but on a different level than the one just recited from Leviticus. This is the only time in the year when kneeling is permitted to the Jew. The Jew does not kneel customarily because that would be a recognition of the divinity of any emperor or kaiser or president who would demand this kind of reverence. There, in this little community with which Franz Rosenzweig worshipped, the entire congregation knelt. Franz Rosenzweig saw for the first time in his life this kind of community addressing itself to God. Something happened to Franz Rosenzweig during the drama of Yom Kippur.

Then the story of Jonah is chanted, the story of the prophet who tried to escape God. He was given a charge to go to Nineveh, the capital city of the Assyrians. You remember that the Assyrians were the archenemy of Israel. They wanted to possess not only Israel but everything in their way. The Assyrians being locked up in Mesopotamia, wanted to reach the great sea, because only then would they be in contact with the world. The Assyrians had a strong and destructive army and Israel was one of the newest neighbors on the list to be destroyed.

God sent a prophet otherwise unknown to us, Jonah, to go out and to preach to the Ninevites to return to the Lord because they had sinned by using destructive military power. If they did not repent, then they would be destroyed. But they had the chance to repent. Jonah said, "They are pagans and men of the sword; it is useless to preach to them." And rather than going East, he bought a ticket to go West. He wanted to go as far West as possible, to Tarshish, which is Marseilles or maybe southern Spain. He thought he would be safe.

But there was a tremendous storm at sea; Jonah's ship was about to sink. The heathen captain asked himself, "What happened? Somebody must have done something wrong." (Although he's a heathen, he still thinks Jewishly; namely, that every misfortune must have a reason.) God, even a pagan God, does not punish without cause, so somebody must be behind this storm.

Lots were drawn, and the lot fell on Jonah. The captain came and asked Jonah, "Who are you? What is your work? Where do you come from and where do you go?" Jonah confessed, "I believe in God," (which he didn't, but he pretended). "I believe in God who made heaven and earth, and I am fleeing before him." The captain asked, "What shall I do with you?" He said, "Throw me overboard."

This is a dramatic story of the conversion of an unwilling prophet who tried to escape God. He was not allowed to escape, even from the big fish (a word usually translated as *whale*). The big fish spat him out on the land, and Jonah reached Assyria. There an unforseen thing happened. The king and his advisors realized that they had done wrong and they decided to return to God. The king issued a decree that everybody should fast for three days. They repented deeply and God had pity on them and did not destroy them.

Then Jonah became very sad and said, "Well, I thought You would destroy them; it may

be useless for me to preach to them and I would
like to die, that's all I want now." And God said,
"Now, why are you so nervous, there's still
meaning in the world." And God added, "How
shall I destroy Nineveh which is a large city with
so many people there and so many animals?"
That's the last line in the text. Even the animals
deserve pity if God is a God of pity and compassion. Franz Rosenzweig heard the recitation of
the book of Jonah on that Yom Kippur.

The evening of Yom Kippur comes on very
soon. The community chants: "Open the gate in
the hour when the gates are being closed, we shall
enter your gates." And then the confession:
"Hear O Israel, The Lord our God, The Lord is
one." And then, "The Lord, he is God," which in
Franz Rosenzweig's interpretation means that the
God of Love is the true God. *Adonai hu ha-
Elohim* according to Rosenzweig means, "the God
of mercy is God." The ram's horn is blown once,
and the day has come to a close. Rosenzweig
witnessed a drama of the contact between God
and us; he partook in the experience of God's
presence.

Rosenzweig came out of the synagogue,
knowing that he could not convert to Christianity.
What he wanted, the experience of the presence of
God, was alive in Judaism; he did not have to
leave Judaism in order to experience the presence
of God. The Christian, Rosenzweig says, has to be
a Christian in order to achieve salvation; the Jew
does not have to become a Christian. Rosenzweig
decided to devote the rest of his life to Judaism,
to its study and, later, to the teaching of Judaism.
He wrote a long letter to his chosen godfather.
Rudolf Ehrenberg was a professor of natural
sciences and in addition a Protestant theologian.
Rosenzweig wrote, "We are wholly agreed as to
what Christ and his church mean to the world:
no one can reach the Father save through him.

But the situation is quite different for one who does not have to reach the Father because he is already with him. And this is true of the people of Israel (though not of individual Jews)." To his concerned mother he wrote: "You will understand, Mother, I remain a Jew."

That's the story of Yom Kippur 1913. This is a very brief introduction to the event which radically changed Franz Rosenzweig. Thank you.

THE ENSUING DISCUSSION

Following Professor Glatzer's address, Rabbi Marx thanked him on behalf of Congregation Solel and Common Ground, attributing the extraordinary experience of the exposure not only to Dr. Glatzer's "intellectual versatility," but also to "his gentle nature." He asked me to open the discussion.

Dr. Miller:
There are several things about Franz Rosenzweig which make him especially interesting to a Christian student of his writings like myself. First of all, he is a Jewish thinker who is able to write about Christianity with a real feel for it from within. I think that you can see from Professor Glatzer's sketch of Rosenzweig's life that he was even waving a New Testament at one point and standing on the brink of baptism. He really went far, not in just studying Christianity intellectually, but feeling it from within. For someone like myself who studies comparative religions, that's a very difficult thing to do. Some people would say it is not achievable at all, or certainly achievable only with great difficulty. Yet that's what Rosenzweig achieved in his study of Christianity. Reading what he writes about Christianity, one knows that he is writing not only with the knowledge he had, but with a feeling for that knowledge. That is most unusual in religious dialogue and most difficult to attain.

Secondly, Rosenzweig's evaluation of Christianity is tremendously generous. Now Judaism, of course, doesn't have a "salvation only in Judaism" doctrine comparable to Christianity's "no salvation outside the Church" theory. We find an early development of the principle of the Noahide covenant, that there is a covenant of the Gentiles with God, and salvation is achievable by non-Jews, though Israel is called to the covenant given through Moses.

Nevertheless, Rosenzweig goes beyond that in his assessment of Christianity. He goes beyond saying that the Christian can be saved, just as any Gentile can be saved, by living righteously. He recognizes Jesus as playing a mediating role for a segment of the Gentile world in bringing that Gentile world to the Father. But as Professor Glatzer mentioned, Rosenzweig said in the letter to the man who was to be his Godfather, his cousin, Rudolf Ehrenberg, that Jesus is a way to the Father for the Gentile world but is not needed as a way to the Father for the Jew, because the people of Israel already exist with the Father in a covenantal relationship.

But it's the other half of that which is especially interesting to me because it is a very generous assessment of Christianity from within Judaism, recognizing a valid covenantal relationship and alluding to a valid religious role being played by Jesus. Jesus is more than a false Messiah, more than an apostate. He becomes someone with a valid religious function vis-a-vis a segment at least of the Gentile world. It's those two issues that I would like Professor Glatzer to speak to in greater detail because I find them especially interesting.

Dr. Glatzer:

What you said, Ron, is that early Judaism created an equal space for the Gentile world. Much is required for a Jew; there are also things required of the Gentile. But if these requirements are fulfilled, the Gentile has an equal share in the world to come, which is the highest distinction Judaism can offer. The seven Noahide commandments include the institution of justice, the prohibition of idolatry, because idolatry includes immorality; there's no exclusion of the Gentile world but rather a granting of a place within the spiritual and the practical order to the world of the Gentile, which is admittedly much, much larger than the world of the Jew. It was very important that you pointed to that. There are many other Talmudic statements which point to that inclusion of the Gentile world. Of course there, too, are reactions to all kinds of evil that happened between Jew and Gentile in the Roman world. It is no wonder that sometimes Jews got quite angry with what was done to them. But beyond that you don't find a hostility against Christianity as such, especially in the third century which was very crucial for the history of Christianity.

What Rosenzweig wanted by way of an understanding between the Jew and the Christian was a greater knowledge between these two. The Jew should know Christianity better than he does, and the Christian should, if he talks about Judaism, know more about Judaism. Rosenzweig was appalled by the ignorance on both sides as far as the other religion is concerned, and he attributed much of anti-Semitism on the one hand, and on the other hand anti-Christian feeling, or anti-Jesus feeling on the part of the Jews, to this lack of knowledge. They just don't know enough. There are misconceptions of Christianity, of the founder of Christianity, but you can't operate on that. That was Franz Rosenzweig's attitude also in other matters. Man is not informed enough and thus things happen as they do. He did not speak explicitly of a dual covenant, but it is implied that once a better understanding is attained between these two communities of faith, things will look different than they look today.

Rabbi Marx:

I want to be personal for just a moment in order to describe a problem that stems from Franz Rosenzweig's writings. When I taught philosophy at DePaul University several years ago, I was continually impressed by the difficulty that these primarily Catholic students had in comprehending what Plato meant by an ideal world. Here were students who had been taught to believe in an ideal world, heaven, who nevertheless found it difficult to comprehend the philosophical basis for such a belief. When Plato talked about the material world of the body, and the ideal world of the soul, he really did believe that the ideal world of the soul was superior to this world in which we labor and live and die. For Plato the world of pure ideas was not only superior, but also ultimately more real than this material world in which we engage in everyday commerce and conflict. Similarly, it is hard to understand how Franz Rosenzweig, though opposed to Hegel, though insisting that Hegel's historical Idealism must be replaced by a concern for the individual, was asserting his own brand of Idealism. In rejecting the man that he had studied and about whom he probably knew more than anyone of his generation, Franz Rosenzweig was creating his own brand of Idealism that affected Judaism in a profound way.

For Rosenzweig's thesis, and it is certainly one that is relevant to the Jewish-Christian dialogue, is that Christianity moves within time but Judaism moves above time. Judaism thus becomes an idea that transcends any experience in which we are involved in this world. For Rosenzweig, the Christian is constantly becoming. Christianity moves from the first Advent, from the first coming of Jesus, toward the Second Coming. The Second Coming of Jesus is the goal. It will be that moment in time in which the promise of the first coming is fulfilled. Now for Judaism none of this is relevant. For Judaism had already arrived at eternity. It had already come to the point to which it was aiming.

Now the best way I can describe this transcendence is by comparing two holidays, a secular one and a religious one--the 4th of July and Passover. In its observance, the 4th of July has nothing to do with the event itself. To be sure, we may watch a television program in which somebody reads from the Declaration of Independence or expresses a patriotic thought, but the event of American Independence is seldom, if ever, built into the observance of the holiday itself. We celebrate it primarily with fireworks.

And how do we observe Passover? "We were slaves." We, we who are observing this now, *we* were slaves in the land of Egypt--and the whole Passover Seder reenacts the event itself. Thus, past and present are united in an experience that transcends time. For Rosenzweig, Judaism has achieved eternity. It is above any considerations of past and future. As a matter of fact, past and future are to be found together in the Passover's reenactment of past suffering and its promise of future redemption. Now how does this provide the groundwork for a dialogue?

Rosenzweig was convinced that Christianity must continue to seek converts, and that Judaism should seek only the Jew. The mission of Christianity is legitimate, but it is not relevant to Jews. An assimilating German Jew would hardly say anything like that. Rosenzweig's answer was the antithesis of what so many German Jews were doing; namely, seeking an amalgamation of Judaism and the Christian environment around them. Rosenzweig said instead that the secret of Judaism is that it is separate and Jews must ever remain apart. Only at the end of time, when Christianity gives up its need to proselytize, will Judaism then give up its need to remain apart. The reconciliation will be through the act of revelation which gives the Jew love. Love is the form through which Judaism and Christianity together express their concern for the world in which they live.

In seeking such a reconciliation, it seems to me that Rosenzweig has created certain problems for us, and I would like to ask Dr. Glatzer to comment on them. In removing a people from history as Rosenzweig did, and in saying that this people rides above the arch of history, where is the incentive for a Jewish involvement in the crucial moral and ethical problems of contemporary life? Rosenzweig, of course, had not experienced the Holocaust, nor the establishment of the state of Israel. Perhaps he cannot be faulted for minimizing the need for an active Jewish involvement in the temporal needs of his people and of humanity at large.

In his latest collection of essays which were published just a few years ago, *Essays on Jewish Thought*, Dr. Glatzer has reminded us that the *Lehrhaus*, the great school Rosenzweig established, never met in any one place. The absence of a central locus was entirely in keeping with a philosophy which sought to picture a religion that transcended time and place.

But in this rejection of time and place Rosenzweig leaves us hungry. And the area in which I feel the hunger is where I perceive the greatest possibility for Jewish-Christian dialogue and that is in the area of justice. To be sure, Rosenzweig thought of the prophets as those who had special insight into the meaning of revelation, but wisdom and insight are hardly surrogates for action. Rosenzweig suggested that justice would be the byproduct of the revelation which emerged on top of another series of relationships: God, man, and the world. The triangle of creation, revelation, and redemption, superimposed upon God, man, and the world, provides a theoretical basis for social action. But justice is difficult to perceive as an abstraction. It is precisely that element of religious thought that requires time and space.

The role of justice, not omitted but expanded, is what we must explore if our dialogue is to become meaningful. "It has been told thee, O man, what the Lord doth require of thee, to do justice, to love mercy and to walk humbly with thy God." (Micah 6:8) Justice is not beyond the essence of this world; it is a crucial part of the essence of this world, just as it is undeniably a product of time. The *Lehrhaus* according to Rosenzweig must be a place where Judaism appreciates and understands its timelessness. The *Lehrhaus* was a place where Jews came to study and then they would come to worship. What we miss in the *Lehrhaus* is a place where Jews, in this world, could seek justice and could act.

Dr. Glatzer:

Rabbi Marx, you are, of course, right in trying to see the lack of the practical aspect of justice in Franz Rosenzweig. However, it is implied in Franz Rosenzweig's writing. When he speaks of redemption, he understands under redemption the translation of the love feeling which a person gains in revelation. He translates it into the love of his fellow human beings by doing justice. Doing justice and love are the fulfillment of what revelation demands of the Jew. They are then part of redemption. That is highly theological, to my taste too much so, but Franz Rosenzweig was bound by his own system. The system forced him into certain categorizations which he otherwise could have fought. But the content is there. He even accepted Socialism, although he was not a socialist. He was a capitalist. How could he avoid being a capitalist? But he accepted Socialism as one of the ways to the Kingdom of God. Here again is the use of theological terminology for something which is not at all theological. Socialism is not theology; it is an economic/political idea. But Franz Rosenzweig accepted that as one of the ways which leads to the desired end. The desired end is redemption and the way to it, one of the ways, is Socialism. Zionism is another of the ways to some other part of his system, although he was not a Zionist. He was not an anti-Zionist but an honest-to-goodness non-Zionist.

What you said was very important, that the Jew should actually try to get back into history. He rightly or wrongly excluded himself or was excluded from history, but he should come back. Of course, now we are fifty years after Franz Rosenzweig's death. What

Rosenzweig would say today we don't know for sure, but in any case he would face a different kind of reality and try to cope with it. But in his time he did speak of this historic rift between Judaism and the Church or the churches.

He saw over and over again the sacred imagery which presents the Church as a beautiful maiden with a staff in her hand and open eyes looking towards the world, and next to her stands another beautiful woman but her eyes are blindfolded. She doesn't see the world; her staff of rule is broken. And this, of course, is the synagogue. Franz Rosenzweig said, "That's it, yes. You think that this is an insult to us; no, I accept that. That is the truth, the historic truth. That's where we are; we don't want to see the world. You say that we are not supposed to see the world; we don't want to see the world. Our staff is broken; we don't want a perfect staff---that means an unbroken rule. The Church has it in the world. We don't want it." It was a tricky answer. The Gentile expected a negative Jewish reaction to the image of the two women. But Franz Rosenzweig said, "Fine. We'll accept it. That might change in the process of time, but for the time being, that's it." That was his way of reacting to what history meant to the Jew of his day, not more than that.

Rabbi Marx

I find that answer so interesting that I want to add a question, and then I know Ron wants to add something. I find it fascinating, Dr. Glatzer, to see the possibility of an evolutionary thought in Franz Rosenzweig. For Franz Rosenzweig the Jewish community was a blood community and that's a very interesting thing for a highly enlightened German Jewish intellectual to say--that one had to be born into the Jewish community. One could join it also, I suppose, by experiencing it. Now at the same time, Franz Rosenzweig was saying and he said it over and over again, "It's a blessing for the Jewish community that it doesn't have land, a blessing that it has only one language for Jews, the Hebrew language." So Franz Rosenzweig wanted everyone to study Hebrew. In other words, what Rosenzweig seems to be saying on the one hand when he talks about land and language is that there's something that transcends anything of this world. But when he talks about blood, that one can only be born into this, he seems to be denying the possibility of an ideal society that is entered through free election. I'd appreciate your commenting on that.

Dr. Glatzer

This too is a reaction against what the world said to the Jew. The other possibility outside of this blood relationship would be conquest. Go out and conquer. That is what Franz Rosenzweig attributes to world history. World history is the history of conquering nations. They go out and conquer parts of somebody else's territory. We don't do that, and so we are out of history; what's left? Family life and continuation via what he calls blood. That has nothing to do with Hitler's stress on blood.

Dr. Miller

One thing that seems to me important to bring up today is what I see as the generosity and humility in Rosenzweig's view of Christianity. You see there's often an attitude of---it's superfluous, if not dangerous, to look at what another religion is doing. And Rosenzweig's attitude is, at least regarding Christianity, that from his perspective, there are things which Christianity does best as there are things that Judaism does best. There are ways in which Judaism and Christianity need each other because they both have a goal that is beyond their own personal agendas, which is to say, they're both instruments of God. For him they don't meet in history, as Professor Glatzer said: they meet beyond history. They work very differently together in history, and neither of them exhausts, so to speak, the will and purpose of God. Now that to me is a very striking attitude toward other religions, because

Christians often grow up with the notion of "no salvation outside the Church," and therefore every other religion is wrong. In Judaism you have the old saw: anything new in Christianity is not true and anything true in Christianity is not new. That's not the way Rosenzweig thought. I find in him an openness to both sides. The Christian can recognize that God is achieving things through the Jews that the Christian is not privy to, either personally or through the Church as a total institution. By the same token there are things that God wants to do through Christianity that the Jew is not privy to. God's purposes are larger than either of the two communities.

I see that as a possible basis for a tremendous kind of growth in religious consciousness today, and I might say through my own experience as a college teacher, it is the only kind of religious perspective that I see as meaningful to many young people today. In other words, as soon as they hear the notion that something worthwhile and meaningful is going on within our four walls and outside of them there is nothing, they perceive that message as a kiss of death to any burgeoning interest in religion because they live in a bigger world and perceive any parochial religious perspective as tending towards the kind of attitude one finds in cults and in the extreme groups on the Religious Right.

Rosenzweig maintains that there would be a need for a Jew to know about Christianity, precisely because it is something, as Professor Glatzer says, willed by God. Not *allowed* by God, not tolerated, or permitted by God as an aberration, but willed by God. Something willed by God merits the study of someone who believes in God. I find an attitude many times, both on the part of Christians and Jews, of why waste time with this other religion? I have so much in my own religion to study, I can never exhaust it in my lifetime, which is, of course, true for all of us. There seems to be a movement today even within Christianity after that first flush of activity in Vatican II to pull back into one's own bailiwick and not look outside. I don't see that as healthy.

Rabbi Marx
You are raising a very serious problem. I study Christianity, but I don't study it the way I study Isaiah or Amos or Deuteronomy. I study it as history, and I study it to learn more about Judaism because through Christianity I can find out more about Judaism. My problem is that if Franz Rosenzweig is correct, there are some very serious breaches between Judaism and Christianity that have to be dealt with. If Christianity's task is continually to seek converts, then conversion is its mission in the world and this is, in essence, to say that non-Christians are wrong and are missing something. It is a put-down. It is an ultimate put-down of the people who are the objects of the conversionary effort. And its consequences can be horrendous in terms of what is going on in this world and the way we treat one another. It is this problem, I think, that Christianity has to address if it is to take Franz Rosenzweig seriously, and if it is to create the conditions for a true meeting in eternity between the two religions.

Dr. Miller
I think that's a good point. I want to make some comments on Rosenzweig's view of conversion. First of all, and I think this is quite obvious by now, he didn't mean that Christians should convert Jews. Secondly, I think that when one looks at Rosenzweig's view of revelation as basically a way of being oriented, a way of having an up and a down, a before and afterwards, a way of being at home, the conversionary dimension of Christianity is not of the crusader model or anything like that, nor is it of the street corner evangelizing model. It is rather that Christianity is legitimate in offering a home, as Martin Buber said, a home to those who are spiritually homeless. That is to say, for people who have no sense of orientation to God, Rosenzweig

believed that Christianity and Jesus could mediate a relationship with the God of Israel. Now the way that relationship is presented can be very flexible. Rosenzweig's point is that Christianity stands in the world as a way to God. When he uses his image of the star, he sees Judaism as the fire at the center of the star and Christianity as the outreaching rays. So in other words, from his perspective, it's legitimate for Christianity to mediate, to offer to people without a spiritual home a relationship to the God of Israel through Christianity. This would not include Jews; it would not include people who had a spiritual home, but it would mean an offering to an otherwise disoriented, alienated group of people.

I wonder, Dr. Glatzer, how you see Rosenzweig's view of Jesus and Paul in the light of this discussion.

Dr. Glatzer
He considered Jesus the redeemer of the Gentile world. And he accepted the definition of the Christian that Jesus is the Son of God; all of us are children of God, that is the biblical idea. In Deuteronomy "you are children of the Lord your God," all of you. And so if the Christian separates Jesus out of the general sonship and focuses on Jesus through a divine attribute, all right, that's the Christian's way of treating history and that's his right. But he criticized, just as Buber criticized, Paul as one who distorted the Jewish heritage while pretending that he preached the Jewish heritage. But Franz Rosenzweig did not go out of his way as Buber did in criticizing in publications the Christian ideology. He didn't do it. He accepted Christianity as an existing truth. If God wanted Christianity to be in the world, Christianity has a role to play in the world. Judaism has a different role. It doesn't mean that we can't cooperate. We can cooperate in establishing a little more justice in the world but theologically there is separation. We'll meet at the end of days.

Rabbi Marx
What do you think Franz Rosenzweig would have to say today about the state of Israel?

Dr. Glatzer:
That's very difficult to answer. One thing we do know is that he realized the importance of the land of Israel during his lifetime. He died in 1929. In the mid-20s, long before the state of Israel was established, there was a small Zionist movement. There were already colonies, settlements in Palestine, and the Hebrew language was already being established there. Franz Rosenzweig liked that very much, but it didn't convert him to Zionism. He said, "If I read that children talk Hebrew to each other and play in Hebrew and then compare our own achievements in going through the grammar and learning the active and the passive and being very glad to master already one third of the basic Hebrew vocabulary, then I say to myself that Tel Aviv is still better than what we have here." So he saw the reality and was very glad for it. He recognized the fact that the Sabbath is theoretically observed by the orthodox in Frankfurt, while in Tel Aviv or Jerusalem the Sabbath is really observed. There is quiet and peace and tranquility. Without becoming a Zionist, he still saw the importance and the achievement of the Zionist endeavors in the land of Israel. You might ask why didn't he then become a Zionist. That would have forced him into acceptance of nationalism, and this he didn't want. Since he rejected German nationalism in the mid-20s, he could not accept any other nationalism.

Rabbi Marx
I just want to add a little footnote to that, in terms of what I get out of Franz Rosenzweig today. It is the idea of holiness. To me *kadosh* (holy) means a combination of two things Franz Rosenzweig was saying to me as I read him. One is separateness and the other is coming together. To me *kadosh* is both.

Everything that is holy is separate: above time and beyond any location. But then it means coming back to time, coming back into space. Rosenzweig wanted to study Hebrew. He said the Bible could only be read in Hebrew. But here he was the same man who had helped Buber translate the Bible into German. But he said the Bible really could be understood only from the inside. What he was ultimately talking about was the idea of a holy, eternal now. One of the articles he published, "Die Zeit Ist" (*The Time Is Now*) demonstrates the sense of a nowness, a presence that surpasses any given moment in history and that has to mean transcending value. And that sense of the holy role that each one of us plays, that sense of the timelessness of each one of us, is something that will always live in Franz Rosenzweig's writing.

Dr. Miller

I agree. And, in summary, I would like to share my own conviction, deepened by the experience of this day, that there has been no Jewish theology about Christianity since Franz Rosenzweig that has been more daring, more radical, or more open. Even though we are talking about the 50th anniversary of his death, if we're talking in terms of theological development, we're still at today. Because if Franz Rosenzweig were here today, he would still be on the growing edge. There's no one who has developed a more far-reaching and provocative thesis about possible relationships between these two faith communities.

Rabbi Marx

Our time is up but the work of the Jewish-Christian dialogue has not ended. We are grateful for this day, for the pioneering work of Franz Rosenzweig, for Dr. Miller's comments, and for Professor Glatzer's presence today. Thank you.

FORMING COMMUNITIES
OF DIALOGUE

The last words of *The Star of Redemption* are "into life." This highlights the existential orientation of Rosenzweig's thought. It is the kind of thought that cries out for embodiment and concretization in lived experience. Rosenzweig's ideas and the whole reality of the *Lehrhaus* were foremost in my mind when I first discussed with a friend and fellow graduate student, Rabbi Marc Gellman, the possibility of a contemporary center for interfaith study and dialogue. Another friend, James Kenney, whose graduate studies focused on the relationship of Eastern thought and Western science, soon joined us in our initial plans, and Common Ground was incorporated on May 7, 1975.

Marc Gellman now has a pulpit in New York and continues to teach and write. Jim Kenney and I are Co-Directors of Common Ground which continues to offer a variety of workshops, retreats, and special events. Many of these have Jewish-Christian dialogue as their focus. It has been my experience that the entry into dialogue proves most problematic. That is where the stereotypes and defenses seem to thrive most vigorously. Through the years I have developed a particular method of working with people in the first stage of dialogue and it is this method, with its underlying principles, that provides the focus of this appendix.

The context is a situation where I have been called in as a resource person for two neighboring religious institutions--a church and a synagogue-- wanting to develop a more dialogical relationship. I meet first with the clergy and eight leaders (four from each group) to discuss both the theory behind an initial event and the concrete details of its implementation. This initial meeting requires at least three hours and is crucial to everything else that will follow.

The principles for the dialogue event are derived from Rosenzweig. The first principle is that dialogue is a journey of discovery, not a duel. This includes the recognition that one's perspective is indeed a per-spective, that truth is beyond adequate articulation, and that revelatory experience transcends propositional formulation. It entails the recognition that truth exists in history and is progressively attained within the dialogue process. The whole process is useless unless the people involved believe that they can learn something from it, that they can indeed grow.

The second principle is that dialogue must be based on self-definition, one's own and one's dialogical partner. Too often we approach the other from our own perspective and fail to allow our dialogical partner the chance to self-identify. "Jews are people who don't believe in Jesus." "Christians are people who hate Jews." These statements will never emerge from self-definition but they are often the starting points of conversations where this principle of self-definition is ignored.

The third principle is receptivity. If dialogue is to proceed from Rosenzweig's motto: *Respondeo etsi mutabor* (I will respond, even if I am changed), then the dialogical partners must accept the fact that they can't prepare ahead of time what they will say. The dialogue must be engaged with a willingness to change. This means being a *Sprachdenker*, one who thinks in the process of dialogical exchange and one who speaks authentically out of that thinking.

A Zen story illustrates the importance of recepti-vity. A rich and self-centered ruler once invited a Zen master to tea. In performing the tea ceremony, the master poured tea into the king's cup until it over-flowed and began to spill down on the floor. "Stop pouring the tea!" shouted the ruler, "the cup is full." "Precisely," answered the master. "Just as the full cup can receive no tea, so can the full mind receive no teaching." Dialogue remains a gesture of futility unless receptivity precedes and accompanies it at every step.

After the theory has been discussed, the concrete details are described. The event requires two evenings, either two consecutive nights or two nights no more than one week apart. One evening is hosted by the synagogue and one by the church. Church and synagogue are to provide forty participants each. The evening begins with a welcome by the host clergy and a tour of the church or synagogue. The participants are then divided into eight groups of ten, each group consisting of five Jews, five Christians, and one of the trained leaders. The clergy and I do not function as group leaders, giving us the freedom to observe the small groups.

The small groups meet for forty minutes. The role of the group leaders is crucial. On the one hand, they are facilitators; on the other hand, they must be firm in keeping the group on target. The task of the first night is self-definition. Each participant finishes the sentence, "What I want to say about myself as a Jew (or Christian) is . . . ." This self-definition is to be accepted without comment or judgment. I consider this the fundamental building block of the ensuing dialogue. Usually there is time to go around the group a second time, allowing for further self-definition. Any remaining time can be used for reactions.

After this small group session, the entire group assembles. At this point I develop one or other of the principles of dialogue, and then both the clergy and I entertain any questions that have arisen about Judaism or Christianity. We then move to some refreshments and informal exchange for the remainder of the evening.

The second night follows a similar pattern, except that the task of the small group changes. Here the sentence to be completed is: "What I as a Jew (or a

Christian) would most like to ask a Christian (or a Jew) is . . . ." The questions vary from "What are those little hats you wear?" to "What do you really believe about those wafers you eat on Sunday?" Here the leader has to make sure that only one person is allowed to answer the question, i.e. one Jew can answer the first question by a Christian, one Christian can answer the next question by a Jew. The beginning and ending of the evening are the same, except that the setting has changed from the church to the synagogue or vice versa.

When the eight leaders first hear about the plan, they sometimes feel that it might be too rigid or structured. I explain, however, that long years of experience have taught me that two types of responses most frequently mar first attempts at dialogue. Some people will use the occasion to deliver long defenses about how they have never been guilty of anti-Semitism (or anti-Gentile feelings). Other people will seize the opportunity to share everything they know or don't know about their own religion and that of their dialogical partner. Neither of these tacks helps dialogue. The highly structured exchange assures each participant's involvement and provides material more geared to a dialogical exchange.

When the second night is over, the people involved generally realize that something significant has happened. At the same time, they are dissatisfied and want more. That dissatisfaction, of course, is ideal and can lead the communities to other kinds of events. A shared Passover Seder might be appropriate or a comparison of Christmas and Hanukkah. Working through a book together and discussing it or an exchange of pulpits might be a next step. The point is that the process has begun and the participants will more than likely want to share it with other members of their respective congregations.

The principles of dialogue that we studied in Rosenzweig's correspondence with his cousin, Hans Ehrenberg, easily translate into programs of dialogue for individuals and communities alike. What works as a leaven among eighty people from two local religious communities can eventually have an impact on the larger religious bodies they represent. Dialogue is not yet characteristic of Jewish-Christian relations, but work towards that level of Jewish-Christian understanding constitutes the greatest tribute we can pay to that model of dialogue, Franz Rosenzweig, the sage of Frankfurt and the subject of this manuscript.

SELECTED BIBLIOGRAPHY

Books

Abbott, Walter M., S.J., ed. *The Documents of Vatican II.* Translated by Very Rev. Msgr. Joseph Gallagher. New York: The American Press, 1966.

Broadt, Lawrence, C.S.P., Helga Croner, and Leon Klenicki, eds. *Biblical Studies: Meeting Ground of Jews and Christians.* New York: Paulist Press, 1980.

Bornkamm, Gunther. *Paul.* Translated by D.M.G. Stalker. New York: Harper & Row Publishers, 1969.

Casper, Bernhard. *Das Dialogische Denken: Eine Untersuchung der religionsphilophischen Bedeutung Franz Rosenzweigs, Ferdinand Ebners und Martin Bubers.* Freiburg: Herder, 1967.

Croner, Helga, compiler. *Stepping Stones to Further Jewish Chistians Relations: An Unabridged Collection of Christian Documents.* New York: Stimulus Books, 1977.

_____, compiler. *More Stepping Stones to Jewish-Christian Relations: An Unabridged Collection of Christian Documents (1975-1983).* New York: Stimulus Books, 1985.

Croner, Helga, and Leon Klenicki, ed. *Issues in the Jewish-Christian Dialogue: Jewish Perspectives on Covenant, Mission and Witness.* New York: Paulist Press, 1979.

Davies, Alan T., ed. *Anti Semitism and the Foundations of Christianity.* New York: Paulist Press, 1979.

Davies, W.D. *Paul and Rabbinic Judaism: Some Rabbinic Elements in Pauline Theology.* New York: Harper Torchbooks, 1948.

Eckstein, Yechiel. *What Christians Should Know About Jews and Judaism.* Waco, TX: Word Publishers, 1984.

Fackenheim, Emil L. *What is Judaism?* New York: Summit Books, 1987.

Fisher, Eugene, J., A. James Rudin, and Marc H. Tanenbaum, eds. *Twenty Years of Jewish-Catholic Relations.* New York: Paulist Press, 1986.

Fox, Matthew, ed. *Western Spirituality: Historical Roots, Ecumenical Routes.* Notre Dame, IN: Fides/Claretian, 1979.

Gaston, Lloyd. *Paul and the Torah.* Vancouver: University of British Columbia Press, 1987.

Glatzer, Nahum N. *Essays on Jewish Thought.* University, AL: The University of Alabama Press, 1978.

_____. *Franz Rosenzweig: His Life and Thought.* New York: Schocken Books, 1961.

Goldstein, Morris. *Jesus in the Jewish Tradition.* New York: The Macmillan Co., 1950.

Goppelt, Leonhard. *Jesus, Paul, and Judaism.* Translated by Edward Schroeder. New York: Thomas Nelson & Sons, 1964.

Hengel, Martin. *Between Jesus and Paul: Studies in the Earliest History of Christianity.* Philadelphia: Fortress Press, 1983.

Horwitz, Gertrude Rivka. *Speech and Time in the Philosophy of Franz Rosenzweig.* Ann Arbor: University Microfilms, Inc., 1974.

Jacob, Walter. *Christianity Through Jewish Eyes: The Quest for Common Ground.* Cincinnati: Hebrew Union College, 1974.

Mayer, Reinhold. *Franz Rosenzweig. Eine Philosophie der dialogischen Erfahrung.* Munich: Chr. Kaiser Verlag, n.d.

Mendes-Flohr, Paul. *The Philosophy of Franz Rosenzweig.* Hanover, NH: University Press of New England, 1988.

Merton, Thomas. *A Vow of Conversation: Journals 1964-1965.* New York: Farrar, Straus, Giroux, 1988.

Miller, Ronald H. *Revelation in Franz Rosenzweig's "The Star of Redemption" and Vatican II's Dei Verbum".* Ann Arbor: University Microfilms, Inc., 1980.

Miller, Ronald H. and James B. Kenney, eds. *Fireball and the Lotus.* Sante Fe, NM: Bear & Co., 1987.

Moses, Stephane. *Systeme et Revelation: La Philosophie de Franz Rosenzweig.* Paris: Editions du Seuil, 1982.

Pawlikowski, John T. and James A. Wilde. *When Catholics Speak About Jews: Notes for Homilists and Catechists.* New York: Liturgy Training Publications, 1987.

Petuchowski, Jakob J., ed. *When Jews and Christians Meet.* Albany, NY: SUNY Press, 1988.

Rahel-Freund, Else. *Franz Rosenzweig's Philosophy of Existence: An Analysis of THE STAR OF REDEMPTION.* The Hague: Martinus Nijhoff, 1979.

Rosenstock-Huessy, Eugen. *Ja und Nein: Auto-Biographische Fraegmente.* Heidelberg: Verlag Lambert Schneider, 1968.

_____, ed. *Judaism Despite Christianity: The "Letters on Christianity and Judaism" between Eugen Rosenstock-Huessy and Franz Rosenzweig.* New York: Schocken Books, 1969.

Rosenzweig, Franz. *Gesammelte Schriften.* The Hague: Martinus Nijhoff, 1979-1984.

_____. *On Jewish Learning.* Edited by N. N. Glatzer. New York: Schocken Books, 1955.

_____. *The Star of Redemption.* Translated by William W. Hallo. Boston: Beacon Press, 1964.

Ruether, Rosemary Radford. *Disputed Questions.* Maryknoll, New York: Orbis Books, 1989.

_____. *Faith and Fratricide: The Theological Roots of Anti-Semitism.* New York: Seabury Press, 1974.

Sanders, E. P. *Paul, the Law, and the Jewish People.* Philadelphia: Fortress Press, 1985.

Sandmel, Samuel. *The First Chrisian Century in Judaism and Christianity: Certainties and Uncertainties.* New York: Oxford Univ. Press, 1969.

Schaeffler, Richard, Bernhard Casper, Shemaryahu Talmon, and Yehoshua Amir. *Offenbarung im Denken Franz Rosenzweig*. Essen: Ludgerus Verlag, 1979.

Schoeps, Hans-Joachim. *Jewish Christianity: Factional Disputes in the Early Church*. Translated by Douglas R. A. Hare. Philadelphia: Fortress Press, 1969.

Scholem, Gershom. *From Berlin to Jerusalem: Memories of My Youth*. Translated by Harry Zohn. New York: Schocken Books, 1980.

Schweitzer, Albert. *The Mysticism of Paul the Apostle*. Translated by B. D. Montgomery. London: A. & C. Black, Ltd., 1931.

Stendahl, Krister. *Paul Among Jews and Gentiles*. Philadelphia: Fortress Press, 1976.

Tewes, Joseph. *Zum Existenzbegriff Franz Rosenzweigs*. Neisenheim am Glan: Verlag Anton Hain, 1970.

Thoma, Clemens. *A Christian Theology of Judaism*. New York: Paulist Press, 1980.

Twersky, Isadore, ed. *A Maimonides Reader*. New York: Behrman House, 1972.

van Buren, Paul M. *A Theology of the Jewish Christian Reality. Part 1: Discerning the Way*. New York: The Seabury Press, 1980.

_____. *A Theology of the Jewish-Christian Reality. Part 2: A Christian Theology of the People Israel*. San Francisco: Harper & Row Publishers, 1983.

_____. *A Theology of the Jewish-Christian Reality. Part 3: Christ in Context.* San Francisco: Harper & Row Publishers, 1988.

Vogel, Manfred. *Quest for a Theology of Judaism.* Lanham, MD: Univ. Press of America, 1987.

Yaffe, Martin David. *The New Thinking of Franz Rosenzweig.* Ann Arbor: University Microfilms, Inc., 1974.

Articles

Rosenzweig, "Atheistic Theology". An English Translation published in *The Canadian Journal of Theology,* Volume XIV, No. 2. Canada: Robert G. Goldy and H. Frederick Holch, 1968.

Cook, Michael J. "The Ties That Bind: An Exposition of II Corinthians 3:12-4:6 and Romans 11:7-10." *When Jews and Christians Meet.* Edited by Jakob J. Petuchowski. Alabany, NY: SUNY Press, 1988.

Gellman, Marc A. "Law and Story in Judaism and Christianity." *Fireball and the Lotus.* Edited by Ronald H. Miller & James B. Kenney. Sante Fe, NM: Bear & Co., 1987.

Miller, Ronald H. "The Spirituality of Franz Rosenzweig." *Western Spirituality: Historical Roots, Ecumenical Routes.* Edited by Matthew Fox. Notre Dame, IN: Fides/Claretian, 1979.

Smith, Mark S. "Jews and Judaism in the Catholic Lectionary." *Fireball and the Lotus.* Edited by Ronald H. Miller and James B. Kenney. Sante Fe, NM: Bear & Co., 1987.

Tanenbaum, Marc H. "A Jewish Viewpoint on Nostra Aetate." *Twenty Years of Jewish-Catholic Relations.* Edited by Eugene J. Fisher, A. James Rudin, and Marc H. Tanenbaum. New York: Paulist Press, 1986.

INDEX

ABOUT THE AUTHOR

Born in St. Louis, Missouri, Ronald H. Miller was educated at St. Louis University, the University of Freiburg im Breisgau in West Germany, the Ratisbonne Center of Jewish-Christian Dialogue in Jerusalem, and Northwestern University in Evanston, Illinois. He has earned five degrees, including a Ph.D. in Comparative Religions. Author of numerous articles and translator of the sermons of Meister Eckhart and the letters of Hildegard of Bingen, he recently co-authored a book with James B. Kenney entitled *Fireball and the Lotus*. Miller and Kenney are the Co-Directors of Common Ground, an adult educational center for religious study and dialogue founded by them in 1975. Dr. Miller has been on the religion faculty of Lake Forest College since 1974 where he is currently Dean of Students and Associate Professor of Religion. He lives in Lake Forest, Illinois with his wife and three children.